JAZZ JUMBLES

MUSICAL CROSSWORDS FOR JAZZ LOVERS

@MOLLYMCMANUS

CHAPTER 1:

JAZZ LEGENDS

DID YOU KNOW THAT LOUIS ARMSTRONG, ONE OF THE MOST INFLUENTIAL FIGURES IN JAZZ HISTORY, WAS SO POPULAR THAT HE RECORDED THE FIRST VERSION OF "WHAT A WONDERFUL WORLD" IN JUST ONE TAKE? DESPITE THE SONG'S INITIAL LUKEWARM RECEPTION IN THE U.S., IT WENT ON TO BECOME ONE OF THE MOST BELOVED JAZZ SONGS WORLDWIDE!

THE PIONEERS OF JAZZ

PAGE 33

ACROSS

1. KNOWN AS THE "FATHER OF THE BLUES."
4. BANDLEADER WHO MENTORED LOUIS ARMSTRONG.
7. COMPOSER OF "IT DON'T MEAN A THING (IF IT AIN'T GOT THAT SWING)."
8. ARRANGER AND BANDLEADER IN THE 1920S, KNOWN FOR HIS WORK WITH FLETCHER HENDERSON.
9. ONE OF THE FIRST IMPORTANT SOLOISTS IN JAZZ, PLAYED THE CLARINET.
10. TROMBONIST WHO RECORDED WITH LOUIS ARMSTRONG.

DOWN

2. "SATCHMO" WAS HIS NICKNAME.
3. OFTEN CREDITED AS THE FIRST JAZZ MUSICIAN, A CORNETIST.
5. PIANIST KNOWN FOR HIS INNOVATIVE PLAYING STYLE, WORKED WITH ARMSTRONG.
6. NICKNAMED "JELLY ROLL," A KEY FIGURE IN EARLY JAZZ.

3

THE BEBOP INNOVATORS

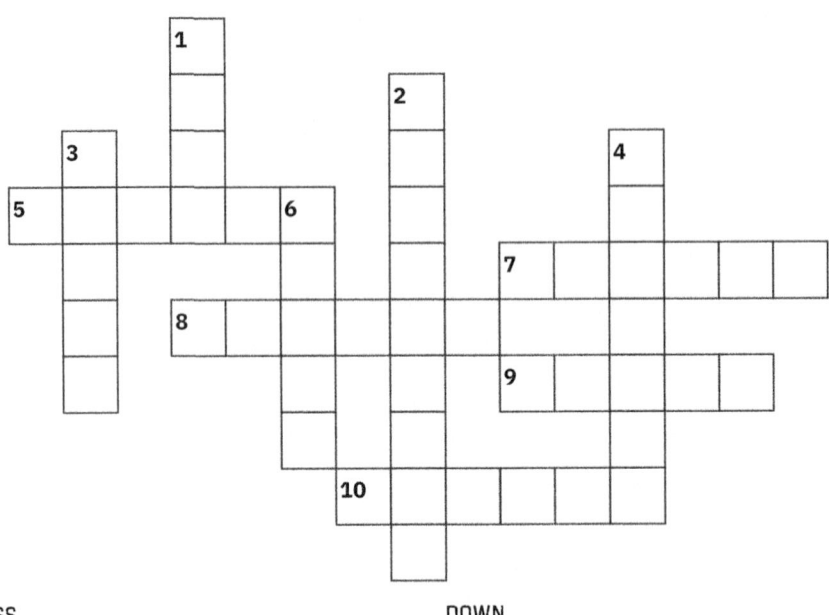

ACROSS

5. SAXOPHONIST NICKNAMED "BIRD," A PIONEER OF BEBOP.
7. BEBOP PIANIST, CONSIDERED ONE OF THE MOST INFLUENTIAL OF HIS TIME.
8. DRUMMER AND BANDLEADER KNOWN FOR HIS POWERFUL PLAYING STYLE IN BEBOP.
9. SAXOPHONIST WHO WAS OFTEN COMPARED TO CHARLIE PARKER.
10. BASSIST AND COMPOSER KNOWN FOR HIS COMPLEX COMPOSITIONS AND BEBOP CONTRIBUTIONS.

DOWN

1. PIANIST AND COMPOSER KNOWN FOR HIS UNIQUE APPROACH TO HARMONY AND RHYTHM.
2. TRUMPETER KNOWN FOR HIS BENT HORN AND BEBOP INNOVATIONS.
3. TRUMPETER WHO WAS PART OF BOTH THE BEBOP AND COOL JAZZ MOVEMENTS.
4. SAXOPHONIST WHO BRIDGED THE SWING AND BEBOP ERAS, KNOWN AS "BEAN."
6. DRUMMER WHO HELPED SHAPE BEBOP, WORKED WITH PARKER AND GILLESPIE.

PAGE 34

MODERN JAZZ ICONS

ACROSS

3. SAXOPHONIST WHO HAS BEEN A PROMINENT FIGURE IN MODERN JAZZ SINCE THE 1990S.
4. BASSIST KNOWN FOR HIS WORK IN BOTH JAZZ AND CLASSICAL MUSIC.
6. SAXOPHONIST KNOWN FOR HIS WORK WITH WEATHER REPORT AND AS A SOLO ARTIST.
7. PIANIST KNOWN FOR HIS UNIQUE BLEND OF JAZZ, CLASSICAL, AND POP INFLUENCES.
8. GUITARIST KNOWN FOR HIS CONTRIBUTIONS TO JAZZ FUSION AND MODERN JAZZ.
10. BASSIST AND VOCALIST WHO WON THE GRAMMY FOR BEST NEW ARTIST.

DOWN

1. SAXOPHONIST KNOWN FOR HIS WORK IN JAZZ FUSION AND AS A SESSION MUSICIAN.
2. TRUMPETER AND BANDLEADER, A LEADING FIGURE IN CONTEMPORARY JAZZ.
5. PIANIST AND COMPOSER, KEY FIGURE IN JAZZ FUSION AND MODERN JAZZ.
9. PIANIST AND COMPOSER KNOWN FOR BLENDING JAZZ WITH FUNK AND ROCK.

JAZZ VOCALISTS

ACROSS

5. JAZZ SINGER WITH A FOUR-OCTAVE VOCAL RANGE, NICKNAMED "SASSY."
6. ALSO KNOWN AS "LADY DAY."
9. JAZZ SINGER AND PIANIST KNOWN FOR HER INVOLVEMENT IN THE CIVIL RIGHTS MOVEMENT.
10. KNOWN AS THE "FIRST LADY OF SONG."

DOWN

1. PIONEERING VOCALIST IN THE STYLE OF VOCALESE.
2. JAZZ SINGER AND CIVIL RIGHTS ACTIVIST, KNOWN FOR HER POWERFUL VOICE.
3. JAZZ SINGER KNOWN FOR HER WORK WITH GENE KRUPA AND INNOVATIVE PHRASING.
4. JAZZ VOCALIST WHO WORKED WITH COUNT BASIE AND OTHER BIG BANDS.
7. LEGENDARY TRUMPETER AND VOCALIST, KNOWN FOR HIS GRAVELLY VOICE.
8. JAZZ SINGER KNOWN FOR HER SOPHISTICATED STYLE AND PHRASING.

THE COOL JAZZ MOVEMENT

ACROSS

2. PIANIST AND COMPOSER KNOWN FOR HIS WORK IN THE COOL JAZZ GENRE.
5. VIBRAPHONIST WHO BLENDED COOL JAZZ WITH LATIN MUSIC.
7. BARITONE SAXOPHONIST KNOWN FOR HIS WORK IN COOL JAZZ.
9. SAXOPHONIST WHO COLLABORATED WITH DAVE BRUBECK, COMPOSER OF "TAKE FIVE."

DOWN

1. SAXOPHONIST KNOWN FOR HIS SMOOTH TONE AND WORK IN COOL JAZZ.
2. TRUMPETER AND VOCALIST, A KEY FIGURE IN THE COOL JAZZ MOVEMENT.
3. SAXOPHONIST WHO WAS PART OF THE "BIRTH OF THE COOL" SESSIONS.
4. TRUMPETER WHO LED THE "BIRTH OF THE COOL" SESSIONS.
6. PIANIST WHO WORKED WITH MILES DAVIS, CONTRIBUTING TO THE COOL JAZZ SOUND.
8. PIANIST AND LEADER OF THE MODERN JAZZ QUARTET, A COOL JAZZ GROUP.

7

CHAPTER 2:

JAZZ INSTRUMENTS AND STYLE

DID YOU KNOW THAT THE SAXOPHONE, NOW A STAPLE IN JAZZ, WAS INITIALLY INTENDED FOR MILITARY BANDS? INVENTED BY ADOLPHE SAX IN 1846, IT WASN'T UNTIL THE EARLY 20TH CENTURY THAT JAZZ MUSICIANS ADOPTED THE SAXOPHONE AND MADE IT ONE OF THE MOST ICONIC INSTRUMENTS IN THE GENRE.

THE JAZZ RHYTHM SECTION

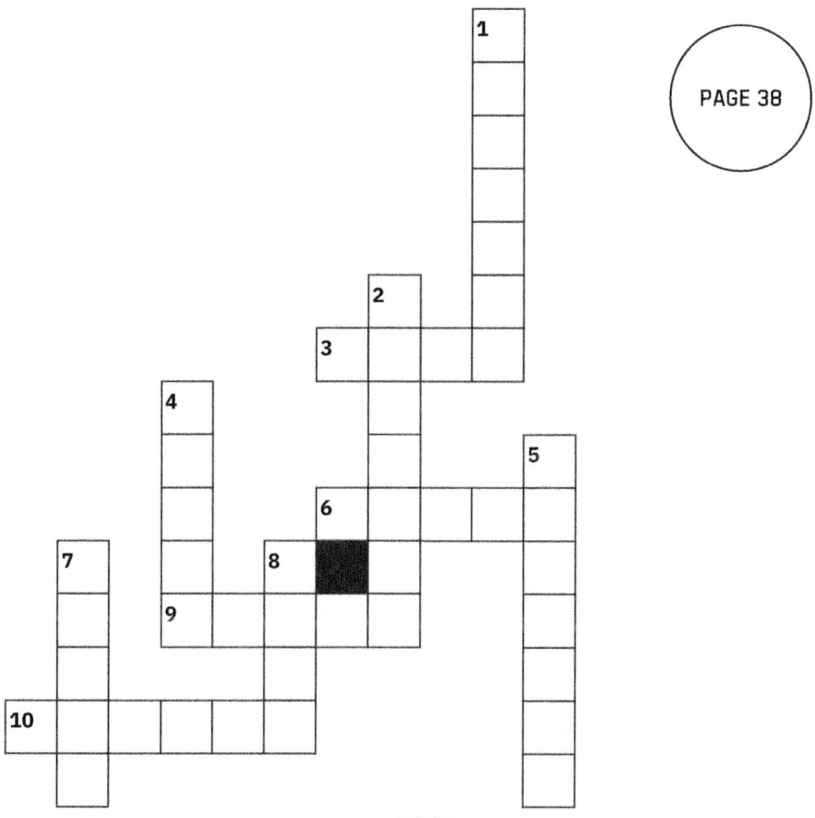

ACROSS

3. INSTRUMENT THAT PROVIDES THE HARMONIC FOUNDATION IN A JAZZ RHYTHM SECTION.

6. INSTRUMENT KNOWN FOR ITS VERSATILITY IN BOTH HARMONY AND MELODY IN JAZZ.

9. A STYLE OF JAZZ CHARACTERIZED BY A STRONG RHYTHMIC GROOVE AND SMOOTH PHRASING.

10. THE OVERALL FEEL OR SWING CREATED BY THE RHYTHM SECTION IN JAZZ.

DOWN

1. DRUMSTICKS WITH BRISTLES, OFTEN USED FOR SOFTER, MORE SUBTLE PLAYING.

2. A BASSLINE TECHNIQUE THAT OUTLINES THE CHORD CHANGES WITH QUARTER NOTES.

4. INSTRUMENT RESPONSIBLE FOR MAINTAINING RHYTHM AND ADDING DYNAMIC ACCENTS.

5. THE PRACTICE OF PLAYING CHORDS RHYTHMICALLY TO ACCOMPANY A SOLOIST.

7. A SET OF NOTES PLAYED TOGETHER, FORMING THE HARMONIC STRUCTURE IN JAZZ.

8. A TYPE OF CYMBAL USED IN JAZZ DRUMMING TO MAINTAIN STEADY RHYTHM.

THE WOODWINDS OF JAZZ

ACROSS

2. A WOODWIND INSTRUMENT COMMONLY ASSOCIATED WITH JAZZ, COMES IN VARIOUS SIZES.
5. A THIN PIECE OF CANE USED TO PRODUCE SOUND IN WOODWIND INSTRUMENTS.
6. A WOODWIND INSTRUMENT SOMETIMES USED IN JAZZ, KNOWN FOR ITS BRIGHT, AIRY SOUND.
8. THE LARGEST COMMON SAXOPHONE, KNOWN FOR ITS LOW, POWERFUL TONE.
9. A POPULAR TYPE OF SAXOPHONE WITH A DEEP, RICH SOUND.
10. A MECHANISM ON WOODWIND INSTRUMENTS THAT OPENS OR CLOSES HOLES TO CHANGE PITCH.

DOWN

1. A WOODWIND INSTRUMENT WITH A SINGLE REED, USED IN EARLY JAZZ AND SWING.
3. A TYPE OF SAXOPHONE, SMALLER AND HIGHER-PITCHED THAN THE TENOR.
4. A HARMONIC PRODUCED ON WOODWIND INSTRUMENTS, CONTRIBUTING TO THE INSTRUMENT'S TONE.
7. A DOUBLE-REED WOODWIND INSTRUMENT, LESS COMMON IN JAZZ BUT SOMETIMES USED.

THE BRASS IN JAZZ

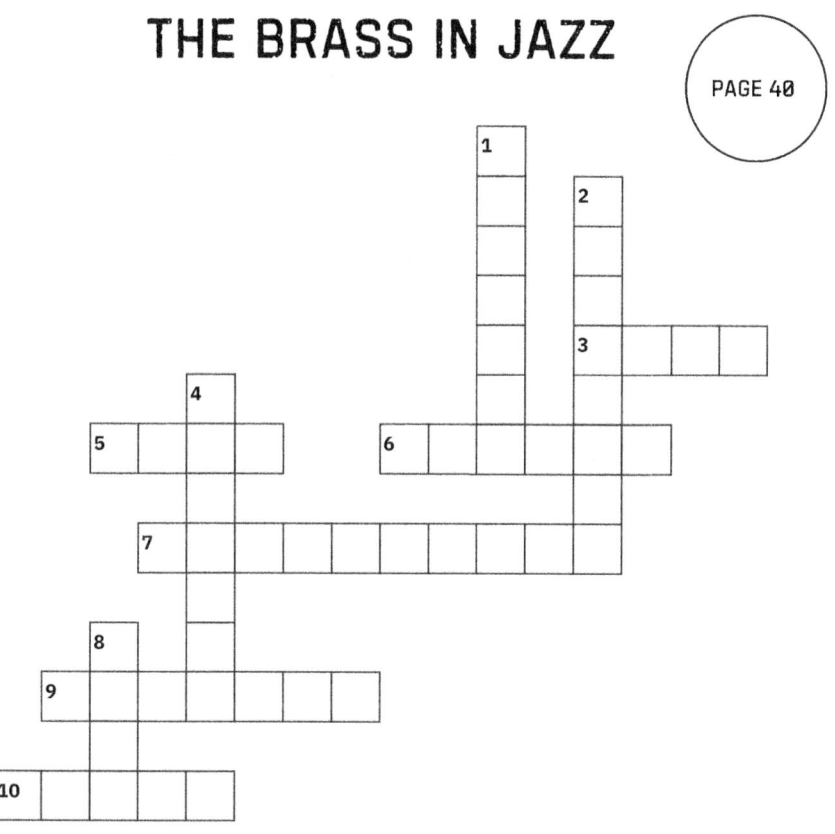

PAGE 40

ACROSS

3. A DEVICE INSERTED INTO A BRASS INSTRUMENT TO ALTER ITS SOUND.
5. A COLLOQUIAL TERM USED FOR BRASS INSTRUMENTS LIKE TRUMPET AND TROMBONE.
6. A TYPE OF MUTE OFTEN USED BY MILES DAVIS TO CREATE A DISTINCTIVE SOUND.
7. THE WAY A MUSICIAN APPLIES THEIR MOUTH TO THE MOUTHPIECE OF A BRASS INSTRUMENT.
9. A GROUP OF BRASS PLAYERS IN A JAZZ BAND, OFTEN INCLUDING TRUMPETS AND TROMBONES.
10. A MECHANISM ON BRASS INSTRUMENTS THAT ALTERS THE PITCH WHEN PRESSED.

DOWN

1. A TYPE OF MUTE THAT RESEMBLES A SINK PLUNGER, USED FOR EXPRESSIVE EFFECTS.
2. A BRASS INSTRUMENT WITH A SLIDE, KNOWN FOR ITS DEEP, RICH TONE.
4. A BRASS INSTRUMENT WITH A BRIGHT, PENETRATING SOUND, WIDELY USED IN JAZZ.
8. THE FLARED END OF A BRASS INSTRUMENT WHERE THE SOUND IS PROJECTED.

JAZZ FUSION

ACROSS

3. THE SPONTANEOUS CREATION OF MUSIC, A HALLMARK OF BOTH JAZZ AND FUSION.
4. REFERS TO INSTRUMENTS LIKE THE ELECTRIC GUITAR AND ELECTRIC BASS USED IN FUSION.
7. REFERS TO THE "MAHAVISHNU ORCHESTRA," A GROUP KNOWN FOR ITS FUSION OF JAZZ AND ROCK.
9. SHORT FOR SYNTHESIZER, AN ELECTRONIC INSTRUMENT USED IN JAZZ FUSION.
10. THE RHYTHMIC FEEL OR SWING, CRUCIAL IN FUSION FOR BLENDING JAZZ WITH OTHER STYLES.

DOWN

1. THE MAIN THEME OR MELODY IN A JAZZ COMPOSITION, OFTEN PLAYED BEFORE AND AFTER IMPROVISATIONS.
2. A TYPE OF BASS GUITAR WITH NO FRETS, OFTEN USED IN FUSION FOR ITS SMOOTH, SLIDING NOTES.
5. REFERS TO CHICK COREA, A KEY FIGURE IN JAZZ FUSION.
6. A STYLE OF JAZZ THAT BLENDS ELEMENTS OF ROCK, FUNK, AND OTHER GENRES.
8. REFERS TO "WEATHER REPORT," A PIONEERING JAZZ FUSION BAND.

LATIN JAZZ

PAGE 42

ACROSS

2. A RHYTHMIC PATTERN ESSENTIAL TO MANY AFRO-CUBAN AND LATIN JAZZ COMPOSITIONS.
5. A PAIR OF SHALLOW DRUMS PLAYED WITH STICKS, OFTEN USED IN LATIN JAZZ.
7. A REPEATED PIANO FIGURE IN LATIN JAZZ, OFTEN USED TO ACCOMPANY SOLOS.
9. A STYLE OF CUBAN MUSIC AND DANCE, INFLUENTIAL IN THE DEVELOPMENT OF LATIN JAZZ.
10. A GENRE OF MUSIC THAT COMBINES ELEMENTS OF LATIN JAZZ, AFRO-CUBAN RHYTHMS, AND DANCE.

DOWN

1. A TALL, NARROW DRUM FROM CUBA, OFTEN USED IN LATIN JAZZ.
3. REFERS TO "AFRO-CUBAN," A BLEND OF AFRICAN AND CUBAN MUSIC STYLES, CENTRAL TO LATIN JAZZ.
4. REFERS TO TITO PUENTE, A LEGENDARY FIGURE IN LATIN JAZZ.
6. REFERS TO "BOSSA NOVA," A STYLE OF BRAZILIAN MUSIC THAT BLENDS SAMBA AND JAZZ.
8. THE SYNCOPATED BASS PATTERN COMMONLY USED IN LATIN JAZZ.

CHAPTER 3:
JAZZ ALBUMS AND SONGS

FUN FACT: DID YOU KNOW THAT MILES DAVIS'S ALBUM "KIND OF BLUE" IS THE BEST-SELLING JAZZ ALBUM OF ALL TIME? RELEASED IN 1959, IT'S OFTEN REGARDED AS THE GREATEST JAZZ ALBUM EVER RECORDED AND WAS INDUCTED INTO THE GRAMMY HALL OF FAME. THE ENTIRE ALBUM WAS RECORDED IN JUST TWO SESSIONS, AND MOST OF THE TRACKS WERE FIRST TAKES!

JAZZ SONG TITLES

ACROSS

1. THE FIRST WORD IN THE TITLE OF A BLUESY TUNE FROM MILES DAVIS'S "KIND OF BLUE" ALBUM.
4. THE FIRST WORD IN THE TITLE OF A JAZZ STANDARD BY WAYNE SHORTER, ALSO THE NAME OF AN ALBUM.
6. THE FIRST WORD IN THE TITLE OF A FUNKY TUNE BY HERBIE HANCOCK FROM HIS EARLY BLUE NOTE RECORDINGS.
7. THE FIRST WORD IN THE TITLE OF A FAMOUS TUNE BY MILES DAVIS FROM THE ALBUM "KIND OF BLUE."
8. THE FIRST WORD IN THE TITLE OF A HARD BOP TUNE BY FREDDIE HUBBARD FROM HIS 1970 ALBUM.
9. A JAZZ PIECE BY LUIZ EÇA, KNOWN FOR ITS LYRICAL MELODY, NAMED AFTER A MARINE ANIMAL.
10. A JAZZ COMPOSITION BY WAYNE SHORTER, OFTEN PLAYED IN A 6/8 TIME SIGNATURE.

DOWN

2. A MODAL JAZZ COMPOSITION BY JOHN COLTRANE, OFTEN ASSOCIATED WITH HIS LIVE PERFORMANCES.
3. A JAZZ COMPOSITION BY CHICK COREA, KNOWN FOR ITS LIVELY RHYTHM AND SPANISH-INSPIRED MELODY.
5. THE FIRST WORD IN THE TITLE OF A BLUES COMPOSITION BY THELONIOUS MONK.

ICONIC JAZZ ALBUMS

PAGE 44

ACROSS

2. THE FIRST WORD IN THE TITLE OF A LANDMARK MILES DAVIS ALBUM FROM 1959.

4. A COLOR-THEMED ALBUM BY JOHN COLTRANE FROM 1957.

6. A LEGENDARY BASSIST AND COMPOSER WHO RELEASED THE INFLUENTIAL ALBUM "AH UM" IN 1959.

8. HIS LIVE ALBUM AT NEWPORT IS ONE OF THE MOST FAMOUS JAZZ PERFORMANCES OF ALL TIME.

9. THE KEY CONCEPT EXPLORED IN DAVE BRUBECK'S GROUNDBREAKING ALBUM FEATURING "TAKE FIVE."

DOWN

1. AN ALBUM BY MILES DAVIS THAT EXPLORES SPANISH THEMES, RELEASED IN 1960.

3. A SPIRITUAL JAZZ ALBUM BY JOHN COLTRANE RELEASED IN 1965.

4. A WORD IN THE TITLE OF A PIONEERING JAZZ FUSION ALBUM BY MILES DAVIS FROM 1970.

5. THE FIRST WORD IN THE TITLE OF JOHN COLTRANE'S REVOLUTIONARY ALBUM FROM 1960.

7. LAST NAME OF THE SAXOPHONIST WHO POPULARIZED BOSSA NOVA WITH AN ALBUM FEATURING "THE GIRL FROM IPANEMA."

16

JAZZ STANDARDS

ACROSS

3. THE FIRST WORD IN A POPULAR JAZZ STANDARD BY COLE PORTER THAT CONTRASTS DAY AND NIGHT.

5. THE FIRST WORD IN A JAZZ STANDARD BY JEROME KERN, OFTEN PLAYED IN MAJOR AND MINOR KEYS.

6. A CLASSIC JAZZ BALLAD THAT HAS BEEN A FAVORITE FOR IMPROVISATION BY JAZZ MUSICIANS.

8. A JAZZ STANDARD FROM AN OPERA BY GEORGE GERSHWIN, OFTEN COVERED BY JAZZ MUSICIANS.

DOWN

1. THE FIRST WORD IN A JAZZ STANDARD FAMOUSLY PERFORMED BY SARAH VAUGHAN AND ELLA FITZGERALD.

2. A FAST-PACED JAZZ STANDARD OFTEN USED AS A TEST PIECE FOR IMPROVISATION.

4. THE FIRST WORD IN A JAZZ SONG POPULARIZED BY FRANK SINATRA THAT TALKS ABOUT THE MOON.

5. THE FIRST WORD IN THE TITLE OF A JAZZ STANDARD OFTEN ASSOCIATED WITH THE FALL SEASON.

7. THE FIRST WORD IN A CLASSIC JAZZ BALLAD BY THELONIOUS MONK.

9. THE FIRST WORD IN THE TITLE OF A POPULAR JAZZ PIECE COMPOSED BY PAUL DESMOND, KNOWN FOR ITS 5/4 TIME SIGNATURE.

THE GREAT COMPOSERS

PAGE 46

ACROSS

1. LAST NAME OF THE COMPOSER WHO MERGED JAZZ WITH CLASSICAL MUSIC IN WORKS LIKE "RHAPSODY IN BLUE."
3. LAST NAME OF THE BASSIST AND COMPOSER KNOWN FOR HIS COMPLEX COMPOSITIONS AND SOCIAL COMMENTARY IN PIECES LIKE "FABLES OF FAUBUS."
5. LAST NAME OF THE COMPOSER OF MANY JAZZ STANDARDS, INCLUDING "ANYTHING GOES" AND "NIGHT AND DAY."
7. LAST NAME OF THE COMPOSER AND PIANIST WHO EXPERIMENTED WITH UNUSUAL TIME SIGNATURES IN PIECES LIKE "BLUE RONDO À LA TURK."
10. LAST NAME OF A JAZZ COMPOSER KNOWN FOR HIS ANGULAR MELODIES AND COMPOSITIONS LIKE "'ROUND MIDNIGHT."

DOWN

2. LAST NAME OF THE PIANIST AND COMPOSER KNOWN FOR INTEGRATING FUNK AND ELECTRONIC ELEMENTS INTO JAZZ WITH ALBUMS LIKE "HEADHUNTERS."
4. LAST NAME OF THE SAXOPHONIST AND COMPOSER WHO WAS A LEADING FIGURE IN THE BEBOP MOVEMENT.
6. LAST NAME OF THE COMPOSER AND BANDLEADER KNOWN FOR "MOOD INDIGO" AND "IT DON'T MEAN A THING (IF IT AIN'T GOT THAT SWING)."
8. LAST NAME OF THE PIANIST AND COMPOSER WHOSE WORK, INCLUDING "WALTZ FOR DEBBY," HAS INFLUENCED GENERATIONS OF JAZZ MUSICIANS.
9. LAST NAME OF THE BRAZILIAN COMPOSER WHO WROTE "THE GIRL FROM IPANEMA," POPULARIZING BOSSA NOVA WORLDWIDE.

LIVE JAZZ RECORDINGS

PAGE 47

ACROSS

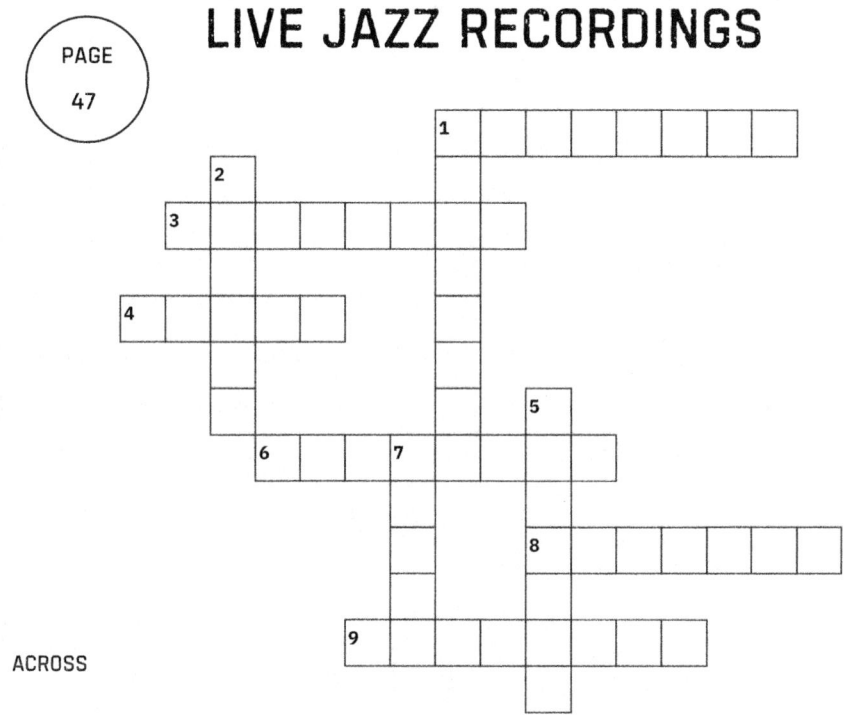

1. THE LAST NAME OF THE SAXOPHONIST WHO RECORDED A LANDMARK LIVE ALBUM AT THE VILLAGE VANGUARD IN 1961.
3. A FAMOUS JAZZ CLUB IN NEW YORK CITY WHERE BILL EVANS RECORDED A LIVE ALBUM IN 1961.
4. THE LAST NAME OF THE BANDLEADER WHOSE PERFORMANCE AT THE NEWPORT JAZZ FESTIVAL IN 1957 BECAME A FAMOUS LIVE RECORDING.
6. A JAZZ FESTIVAL IN CALIFORNIA WHERE THELONIOUS MONK GAVE A MEMORABLE PERFORMANCE, LATER RELEASED AS A LIVE ALBUM.
8. A WORD FROM THE TITLE OF A LIVE ALBUM BY MILES DAVIS, RECORDED AT THE FILLMORE EAST.
9. A SWISS JAZZ FESTIVAL WHERE ELLA FITZGERALD'S LIVE PERFORMANCE WAS CAPTURED ON A CELEBRATED ALBUM.

DOWN

1. A PRESTIGIOUS CONCERT HALL IN NEW YORK CITY WHERE BENNY GOODMAN PERFORMED A LEGENDARY JAZZ CONCERT IN 1938.
2. A FAMOUS LIVE JAZZ RECORDING VENUE IN TORONTO WHERE A HISTORIC JAZZ CONCERT TOOK PLACE IN 1953.
5. THE LOCATION OF A FAMOUS JAZZ FESTIVAL WHERE DUKE ELLINGTON REVIVED HIS CAREER WITH A HISTORIC 1956 PERFORMANCE.
7. A CITY WHERE MILES DAVIS RECORDED A LIVE ALBUM FEATURING HIS 1964 QUINTET.

19

CHAPTER 4:

JAZZ HISTORY AND CULTURE

FUN FACT: DID YOU KNOW THAT DURING THE 1920S, JAZZ MUSIC WAS SO POPULAR THAT IT BECAME KNOWN AS "THE JAZZ AGE"? THIS ERA, ALSO CALLED THE ROARING TWENTIES, SAW JAZZ SPREAD FROM ITS ROOTS IN NEW ORLEANS TO CITIES LIKE CHICAGO AND NEW YORK, INFLUENCING EVERYTHING FROM DANCE STYLES TO FASHION AND BECOMING THE SOUNDTRACK OF A GENERATION!

THE BIRTH OF JAZZ

PAGE 48

ACROSS

2. THE FIRST WORD IN THE NAME OF THE CITY WHERE JAZZ IS OFTEN SAID TO HAVE ORIGINATED.
4. THE RED-LIGHT DISTRICT IN NEW ORLEANS WHERE EARLY JAZZ MUSICIANS OFTEN PERFORMED.
6. THE CITY WHERE JAZZ MUSIC BEGAN TO FLOURISH IN THE EARLY 20TH CENTURY.
7. RELIGIOUS SONGS THAT INFLUENCED EARLY JAZZ AND BLUES, OFTEN SUNG BY AFRICAN AMERICAN COMMUNITIES.
8. A PRECURSOR TO JAZZ, THIS PIANO-BASED MUSIC STYLE WAS POPULAR IN THE LATE 19TH AND EARLY 20TH CENTURIES.
9. A STYLE OF JAZZ THAT ORIGINATED IN NEW ORLEANS, CHARACTERIZED BY A COLLECTIVE IMPROVISATION.

DOWN

1. A CULTURAL GROUP IN NEW ORLEANS WHOSE MUSICAL TRADITIONS CONTRIBUTED TO THE BIRTH OF JAZZ.
3. A GENRE OF MUSIC THAT GREATLY INFLUENCED THE DEVELOPMENT OF JAZZ, CHARACTERIZED BY ITS 12-BAR STRUCTURE.
4. A RHYTHMIC CONCEPT WHERE THE EMPHASIS IS PLACED ON THE OFF-BEATS, A KEY ELEMENT IN JAZZ.
5. A TYPE OF BAND THAT WAS CENTRAL TO THE EARLY DEVELOPMENT OF JAZZ IN NEW ORLEANS.

JAZZ IN THE 1920S

ACROSS

3. THE NAME OF A FAMOUS JAZZ CLUB IN HARLEM WHERE DUKE ELLINGTON AND OTHER LEGENDS PERFORMED.
5. THE U.S. LAW THAT BANNED ALCOHOL IN THE 1920S, LEADING TO THE RISE OF SPEAKEASIES WHERE JAZZ THRIVED.
6. AN ILLEGAL BAR DURING PROHIBITION WHERE JAZZ MUSIC WAS OFTEN PLAYED.
7. THE LAST NAME OF THE TRUMPETER WHO BECAME ONE OF THE MOST INFLUENTIAL FIGURES IN JAZZ DURING THE 1920S.
8. A JAZZ COMPOSER AND BANDLEADER WHO ROSE TO FAME DURING THE 1920S.
9. A NEW YORK NEIGHBORHOOD THAT BECAME THE EPICENTER OF JAZZ CULTURE IN THE 1920S.

DOWN

1. A TERM USED TO DESCRIBE THE 1920S, AN ERA MARKED BY ECONOMIC PROSPERITY AND CULTURAL CHANGE, INCLUDING THE RISE OF JAZZ.
2. A TERM FOR THE YOUNG, FASHIONABLE WOMEN OF THE 1920S WHO WERE OFTEN ASSOCIATED WITH JAZZ CLUBS.
3. A CITY THAT BECAME A MAJOR HUB FOR JAZZ MUSICIANS AFTER MANY MIGRATED FROM NEW ORLEANS.
4. THE CULTURAL MOVEMENT IN HARLEM DURING THE 1920S THAT GREATLY INFLUENCED JAZZ.

JAZZ CLUBS AND VENUES

PAGE 50

ACROSS

1. THE SECOND WORD IN THE NAME OF THE ICONIC JAZZ CLUB IN GREENWICH VILLAGE.
4. A HISTORIC THEATER IN HARLEM KNOWN FOR ITS JAZZ AND SOUL MUSIC PERFORMANCES.
6. A PRESTIGIOUS CONCERT HALL IN NEW YORK WHERE BENNY GOODMAN PLAYED A FAMOUS JAZZ CONCERT.
7. A FAMOUS NEW YORK JAZZ CLUB NAMED AFTER CHARLIE PARKER, KNOWN AS "BIRD."
8. THE SECOND WORD IN THE NAME OF THE ICONIC JAZZ CLUB IN GREENWICH VILLAGE.

DOWN

1. THE FIRST WORD IN THE NAME OF A FAMOUS JAZZ CLUB IN NEW YORK'S GREENWICH VILLAGE.
2. A RHODE ISLAND JAZZ FESTIVAL VENUE WHERE DUKE ELLINGTON REVITALIZED HIS CAREER IN 1956.
3. THE FIRST WORD IN THE NAME OF A FAMOUS HARLEM CLUB WHERE MANY JAZZ LEGENDS PERFORMED.
5. A JAZZ CLUB IN HARLEM THAT WAS A BIRTHPLACE OF THE BEBOP MOVEMENT.
7. THE FIRST WORD IN THE NAME OF A FAMOUS JAZZ CLUB IN NEW YORK, KNOWN FOR ITS BLUE-THEMED DECOR.

JAZZ FESTIVALS

PAGE 51

ACROSS

3. THE FIRST WORD IN THE NAME OF A FAMOUS JAZZ FESTIVAL HELD IN CHICAGO SINCE 1959.
5. A DUTCH CITY WHERE THE NORTH SEA JAZZ FESTIVAL WAS ORIGINALLY HELD.
7. AN ITALIAN REGION KNOWN FOR ITS ANNUAL JAZZ FESTIVAL, ONE OF EUROPE'S MOST PRESTIGIOUS.
9. THE RHODE ISLAND FESTIVAL WHERE DUKE ELLINGTON MADE A HISTORIC COMEBACK IN 1956.
10. A FRENCH TOWN KNOWN FOR ITS ANNUAL JAZZ FESTIVAL IN A ROMAN AMPHITHEATER.

DOWN

1. A CALIFORNIA JAZZ FESTIVAL KNOWN FOR ITS DIVERSE LINE-UP AND OUTDOOR SETTING.
2. THE SECOND WORD IN THE NAME OF THE JAZZ FESTIVAL HELD ANNUALLY IN SEATTLE.
4. A FINNISH CITY THAT HOSTS ONE OF THE OLDEST AND MOST RENOWNED JAZZ FESTIVALS IN EUROPE.
6. THE CITY IN ITALY WHERE THE UMBRIA JAZZ FESTIVAL IS HELD EVERY SUMMER.
8. A FAMOUS JAZZ FESTIVAL HELD ANNUALLY IN SWITZERLAND ON THE SHORES OF LAKE GENEVA.

24

JAZZ AND CINEMA

PAGE 52

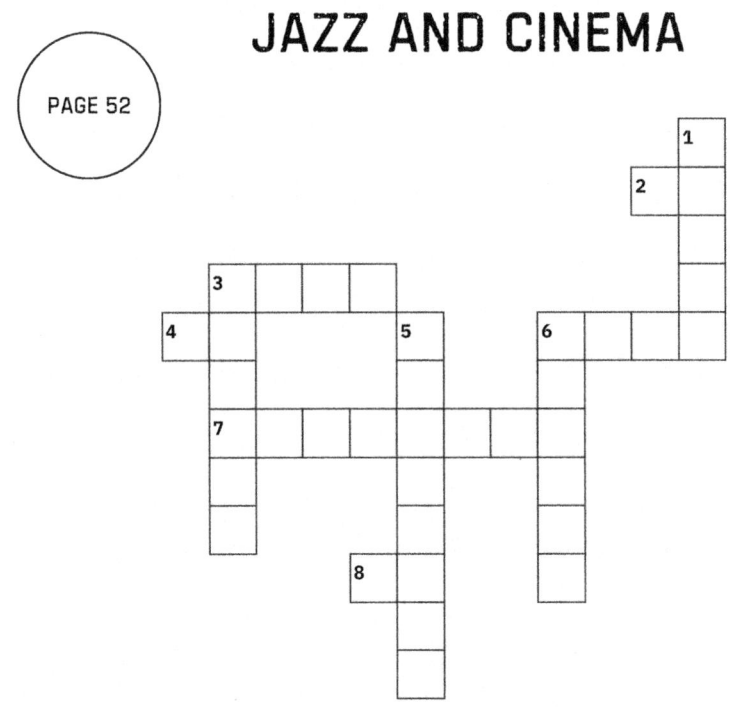

ACROSS

2. THE FIRST WORD IN THE TITLE OF A SPIKE LEE FILM CENTERED AROUND JAZZ AND A FAMILY IN BROOKLYN.

3. THE FIRST WORD IN THE TITLE OF A JAZZ CONCERT FILM BY BERT STERN, DOCUMENTING THE 1958 NEWPORT JAZZ FESTIVAL.

4. THE SECOND WORD IN THE TITLE OF THE 2016 FILM MENTIONED ABOVE.

6. A BIOGRAPHICAL FILM DIRECTED BY CLINT EASTWOOD ABOUT THE LIFE OF CHARLIE PARKER.

7. THE SECOND WORD IN THE TITLE OF A 1986 FILM ABOUT A JAZZ SAXOPHONIST IN PARIS.

8. THE FIRST WORD IN THE TITLE OF A 2016 FILM THAT PAYS HOMAGE TO JAZZ MUSIC AND HOLLYWOOD MUSICALS.

DOWN

1. THE FIRST WORD IN THE TITLE OF A MOVIE ABOUT A JAZZ MUSICIAN STRUGGLING WITH ADDICTION, STARRING DEXTER GORDON.

3. A JAZZ OPERA FILM BY OTTO PREMINGER, STARRING DOROTHY DANDRIDGE AND HARRY BELAFONTE.

5. A FILM ABOUT A YOUNG DRUMMER AND HIS INTENSE JAZZ INSTRUCTOR, RELEASED IN 2014.

6. THE FIRST WORD IN THE TITLE OF A 1984 FILM THAT TELLS THE STORY OF A JAZZ MUSICIAN AND HIS RELATIONSHIP WITH A SINGER.

CHAPTER 5:

JAZZ AROUND THE WORLD

FUN FACT: DID YOU KNOW THAT JAZZ MUSIC HAS A UNIQUE ABILITY TO ADAPT AND BLEND WITH LOCAL MUSICAL TRADITIONS? IN JAPAN, JAZZ IS SO POPULAR THAT THE COUNTRY HAS ITS OWN "JAZZ KISSA" CULTURE-CAFES WHERE PEOPLE GATHER TO LISTEN TO RARE JAZZ RECORDS. MEANWHILE, IN BRAZIL, THE BOSSA NOVA MOVEMENT COMBINED THE RHYTHMS OF SAMBA WITH JAZZ HARMONIES, CREATING A GENRE THAT GAINED GLOBAL POPULARITY IN THE 1960S!

EUROPEAN JAZZ

PAGE 53

ACROSS

2. THE CITY WHERE AMERICAN JAZZ MUSICIANS LIKE SIDNEY BECHET AND JOSEPHINE BAKER FOUND FAME IN THE 1920S.

4. THE STYLE OF JAZZ ASSOCIATED WITH DJANGO REINHARDT, ALSO KNOWN AS GYPSY JAZZ.

5. THE LAST NAME OF THE BELGIAN SINGER-SONGWRITER WHOSE MUSIC OFTEN INCORPORATED JAZZ ELEMENTS.

6. THE LAST NAME OF THE AMERICAN JAZZ SAXOPHONIST WHO BECAME A PROMINENT FIGURE IN EUROPEAN JAZZ EDUCATION.

8. A SWISS CITY KNOWN FOR ITS FAMOUS JAZZ FESTIVAL ON THE SHORES OF LAKE GENEVA.

DOWN

1. THE FIRST NAME OF THE FAMOUS SINGER SIMONE, WHO SPENT MUCH OF HER LATER CAREER IN EUROPE.

2. THE LAST NAME OF THE CANADIAN JAZZ PIANIST WHO WAS A STAPLE IN EUROPEAN JAZZ FESTIVALS.

3. THE FIRST NAME OF THE BRITISH SAXOPHONIST HAYES, A PIONEER OF MODERN JAZZ IN THE UK.

5. THE LAST NAME OF THE AMERICAN SAXOPHONIST MICHAEL, WHO FREQUENTLY COLLABORATED WITH EUROPEAN JAZZ ARTISTS.

7. THE FIRST NAME OF THE LEGENDARY GYPSY JAZZ GUITARIST REINHARDT.

LATIN AMERICAN

ACROSS

2. THE LAST NAME OF THE BRAZILIAN COMPOSER WHO WROTE "THE GIRL FROM IPANEMA."
6. THE FIRST NAME OF THE CUBAN PERCUSSIONIST POZO, WHO COLLABORATED WITH DIZZY GILLESPIE.
7. THE FIRST NAME OF THE LEGENDARY LATIN JAZZ MUSICIAN PUENTE, KNOWN FOR HIS MASTERY OF THE TIMBALES.
8. A STYLE OF BRAZILIAN MUSIC THAT BLENDS SAMBA RHYTHMS WITH JAZZ HARMONY.
9. THE FIRST PART OF A TERM DESCRIBING THE BLEND OF AFRICAN AND CUBAN MUSIC THAT HEAVILY INFLUENCES LATIN JAZZ.

DOWN

1. ANOTHER TERM FOR THE CONGA DRUM, OFTEN USED IN LATIN JAZZ.
3. A TALL, NARROW DRUM FROM CUBA, COMMONLY USED IN LATIN JAZZ.
4. A BRAZILIAN DANCE AND MUSIC STYLE THAT HAS INFLUENCED MANY JAZZ MUSICIANS.
5. THE NICKNAME OF THE ARGENTINE SAXOPHONIST BARBIERI, FAMOUS FOR HIS LATIN JAZZ RECORDINGS.
6. A RHYTHMIC PATTERN ESSENTIAL TO AFRO-CUBAN MUSIC AND LATIN JAZZ.

AFRICAN JAZZ

ACROSS

2. THE FIRST NAME OF THE NIGERIAN MUSICIAN KUTI, WHO BLENDED JAZZ WITH AFRICAN RHYTHMS TO CREATE AFROBEAT.
5. THE LAST NAME OF THE SOUTH AFRICAN TRUMPETER WHO BECAME AN INTERNATIONAL JAZZ STAR.
8. A SOUTH AFRICAN MUSIC STYLE THAT INFLUENCED THE DEVELOPMENT OF JAZZ IN THE COUNTRY.
9. A TOWNSHIP IN SOUTH AFRICA KNOWN FOR ITS JAZZ MUSICIANS AND RICH MUSICAL HERITAGE.
10. A MOUNTAIN IN TANZANIA THAT INSPIRED A FAMOUS JAZZ TUNE BY THE JAZZ MESSENGERS.

DOWN

1. THE FIRST WORD IN THE NAME OF THE SOUTH AFRICAN CITY WITH A VIBRANT JAZZ SCENE.
3. THE FIRST PART OF A TERM USED TO DESCRIBE THE UNIQUE JAZZ STYLE THAT DEVELOPED IN ETHIOPIA.
4. THE LAST NAME OF THE AUSTRIAN KEYBOARDIST JOE, WHO INCORPORATED AFRICAN RHYTHMS INTO HIS MUSIC WITH WEATHER REPORT.
6. THE LAST NAME OF THE AMERICAN JAZZ SINGER WHO DREW INSPIRATION FROM AFRICAN MUSIC AND RHYTHMS.
7. A WEST AFRICAN STRINGED INSTRUMENT, SOMETIMES USED IN JAZZ FUSION.

ASIAN JAZZ FUSION

ACROSS

2. THE LAST NAME OF THE JAPANESE PIANIST HIROMI, KNOWN FOR HER BLEND OF JAZZ, CLASSICAL, AND ROCK.

7. A CITY IN CHINA THAT BECAME A HOTSPOT FOR JAZZ IN THE 1930S.

8. THE FIRST NAME OF THE JAPANESE JAZZ PIANIST AKIYOSHI, WHO FORMED A BIG BAND IN THE UNITED STATES.

9. A TRADITIONAL ENSEMBLE MUSIC FROM INDONESIA, SOMETIMES BLENDED WITH JAZZ ELEMENTS.

10. THE FIRST NAME OF THE JAPANESE SAXOPHONIST WATANABE, A PIONEER OF JAZZ IN ASIA.

DOWN

1. A PAIR OF DRUMS FROM INDIA, OFTEN USED IN JAZZ FUSION.

3. THE FIRST WORD IN THE TITLE OF A POPULAR JAZZ TUNE BY THELONIOUS MONK, INSPIRED BY EASTERN MUSIC.

4. THE CAPITAL OF SOUTH KOREA, WHERE A VIBRANT JAZZ SCENE HAS DEVELOPED.

5. THE LAST NAME OF THE INDIAN SITAR MAESTRO WHO INFLUENCED JAZZ MUSICIANS LIKE JOHN COLTRANE.

6. A TRADITIONAL JAPANESE STRINGED INSTRUMENT SOMETIMES INCORPORATED INTO JAZZ.

JAZZ IN AUSTRALIA AND NEW ZEALAND

PAGE 57

ACROSS

4. THE FIRST NAME OF THE INDIGENOUS AUSTRALIAN MUSICIAN WHO INCORPORATED JAZZ ELEMENTS INTO HIS MUSIC.
6. THE AUSTRALIAN CITY THAT HOSTS ONE OF THE COUNTRY'S BIGGEST JAZZ FESTIVALS.
8. THE CAPITAL OF NEW ZEALAND, KNOWN FOR ITS VIBRANT MUSIC AND ARTS SCENE, INCLUDING JAZZ.
9. A TERM OFTEN ASSOCIATED WITH AUSTRALIA, SOMETIMES USED IN JAZZ COMPOSITIONS TO EVOKE THE VAST, REMOTE INTERIOR OF THE COUNTRY.

DOWN

1. AN AUSTRALIAN CITY KNOWN FOR ITS ANNUAL JAZZ FESTIVAL, ATTRACTING INTERNATIONAL ARTISTS.
2. THE LAST NAME OF THE AUSTRALIAN MULTI-INSTRUMENTALIST JAMES, KNOWN FOR HIS CONTRIBUTIONS TO JAZZ.
3. A CITY IN NEW ZEALAND THAT HOSTS A PROMINENT JAZZ FESTIVAL EACH YEAR.
5. THE LAST NAME OF THE AUSTRALIAN JAZZ MUSICIAN GRAEME, CONSIDERED A PIONEER OF TRADITIONAL JAZZ IN AUSTRALIA.
7. THE ACRONYM REPRESENTING THE COLLABORATION BETWEEN AUSTRALIAN AND NEW ZEALAND MUSICIANS, INCLUDING IN JAZZ.
10. A NICKNAME FOR SOMEONE FROM NEW ZEALAND, A COUNTRY WITH A GROWING JAZZ SCENE.

31

CHAPTER 6:
ANSWERS

THE PIONEERS OF JAZZ

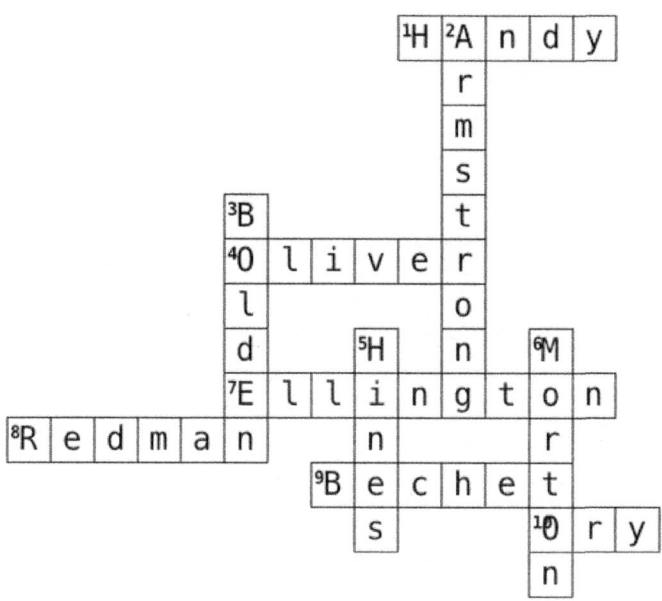

ACROSS

1. KNOWN AS THE "FATHER OF THE BLUES."
4. BANDLEADER WHO MENTORED LOUIS ARMSTRONG.
7. COMPOSER OF "IT DON'T MEAN A THING (IF IT AIN'T GOT THAT SWING)."
8. ARRANGER AND BANDLEADER IN THE 1920S, KNOWN FOR HIS WORK WITH FLETCHER HENDERSON.
9. ONE OF THE FIRST IMPORTANT SOLOISTS IN JAZZ, PLAYED THE CLARINET.
10. TROMBONIST WHO RECORDED WITH LOUIS ARMSTRONG.

DOWN

2. "SATCHMO" WAS HIS NICKNAME.
3. OFTEN CREDITED AS THE FIRST JAZZ MUSICIAN, A CORNETIST.
5. PIANIST KNOWN FOR HIS INNOVATIVE PLAYING STYLE, WORKED WITH ARMSTRONG.
6. NICKNAMED "JELLY ROLL," A KEY FIGURE IN EARLY JAZZ.

THE BEBOP INNOVATORS

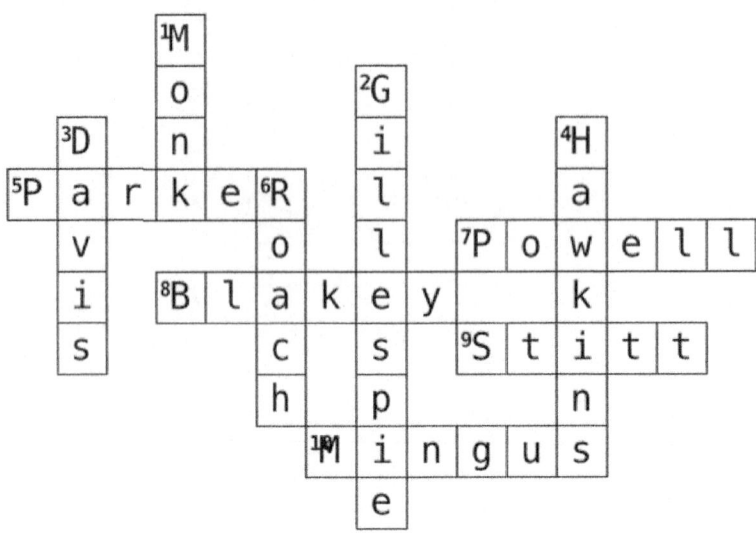

ACROSS

5. SAXOPHONIST NICKNAMED "BIRD," A PIONEER OF BEBOP.
7. BEBOP PIANIST, CONSIDERED ONE OF THE MOST INFLUENTIAL OF HIS TIME.
8. DRUMMER AND BANDLEADER KNOWN FOR HIS POWERFUL PLAYING STYLE IN BEBOP.
9. SAXOPHONIST WHO WAS OFTEN COMPARED TO CHARLIE PARKER.
10. BASSIST AND COMPOSER KNOWN FOR HIS COMPLEX COMPOSITIONS AND BEBOP CONTRIBUTIONS.

DOWN

1. PIANIST AND COMPOSER KNOWN FOR HIS UNIQUE APPROACH TO HARMONY AND RHYTHM.
2. TRUMPETER KNOWN FOR HIS BENT HORN AND BEBOP INNOVATIONS.
3. TRUMPETER WHO WAS PART OF BOTH THE BEBOP AND COOL JAZZ MOVEMENTS.
4. SAXOPHONIST WHO BRIDGED THE SWING AND BEBOP ERAS, KNOWN AS "BEAN."
6. DRUMMER WHO HELPED SHAPE BEBOP, WORKED WITH PARKER AND GILLESPIE.

MODERN JAZZ ICONS

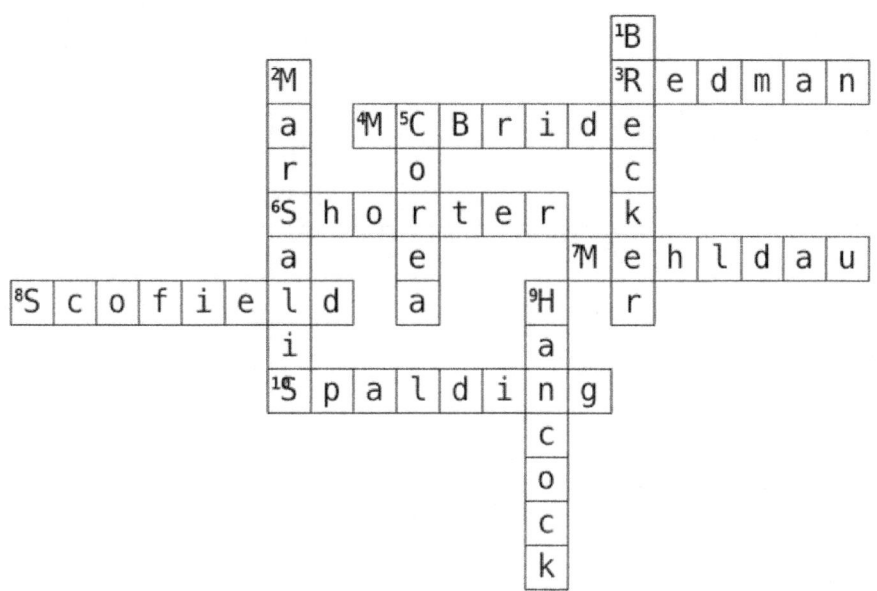

ACROSS

3. SAXOPHONIST WHO HAS BEEN A PROMINENT FIGURE IN MODERN JAZZ SINCE THE 1990S.
4. BASSIST KNOWN FOR HIS WORK IN BOTH JAZZ AND CLASSICAL MUSIC.
6. SAXOPHONIST KNOWN FOR HIS WORK WITH WEATHER REPORT AND AS A SOLO ARTIST.
7. PIANIST KNOWN FOR HIS UNIQUE BLEND OF JAZZ, CLASSICAL, AND POP INFLUENCES.
8. GUITARIST KNOWN FOR HIS CONTRIBUTIONS TO JAZZ FUSION AND MODERN JAZZ.
10. BASSIST AND VOCALIST WHO WON THE GRAMMY FOR BEST NEW ARTIST.

DOWN

1. SAXOPHONIST KNOWN FOR HIS WORK IN JAZZ FUSION AND AS A SESSION MUSICIAN.
2. TRUMPETER AND BANDLEADER, A LEADING FIGURE IN CONTEMPORARY JAZZ.
5. PIANIST AND COMPOSER, KEY FIGURE IN JAZZ FUSION AND MODERN JAZZ.
9. PIANIST AND COMPOSER KNOWN FOR BLENDING JAZZ WITH FUNK AND ROCK.

JAZZ VOCALISTS

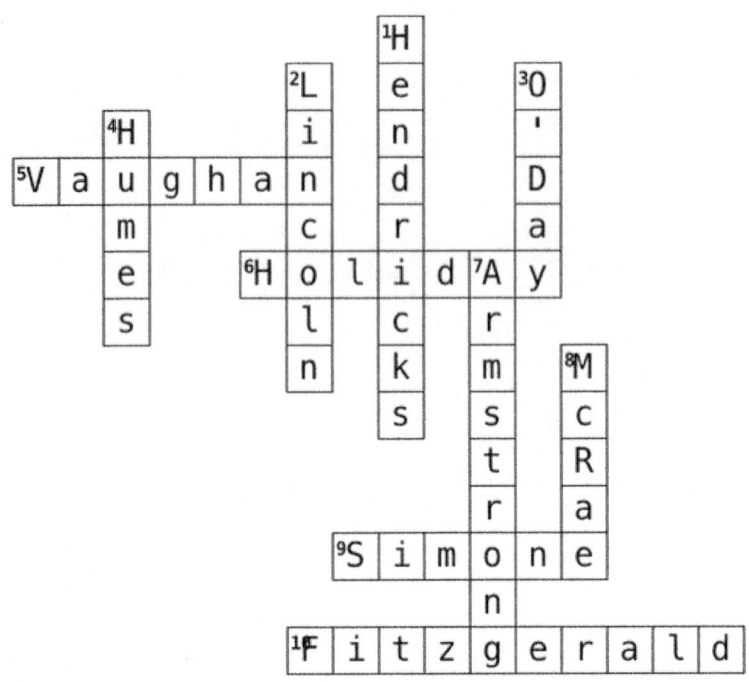

ACROSS

5. JAZZ SINGER WITH A FOUR-OCTAVE VOCAL RANGE, NICKNAMED "SASSY."
6. ALSO KNOWN AS "LADY DAY."
9. JAZZ SINGER AND PIANIST KNOWN FOR HER INVOLVEMENT IN THE CIVIL RIGHTS MOVEMENT.
10. KNOWN AS THE "FIRST LADY OF SONG."

DOWN

1. PIONEERING VOCALIST IN THE STYLE OF VOCALESE.
2. JAZZ SINGER AND CIVIL RIGHTS ACTIVIST, KNOWN FOR HER POWERFUL VOICE.
3. JAZZ SINGER KNOWN FOR HER WORK WITH GENE KRUPA AND INNOVATIVE PHRASING.
4. JAZZ VOCALIST WHO WORKED WITH COUNT BASIE AND OTHER BIG BANDS.
7. LEGENDARY TRUMPETER AND VOCALIST, KNOWN FOR HIS GRAVELLY VOICE.
8. JAZZ SINGER KNOWN FOR HER SOPHISTICATED STYLE AND PHRASING.

THE COOL JAZZ MOVEMENT

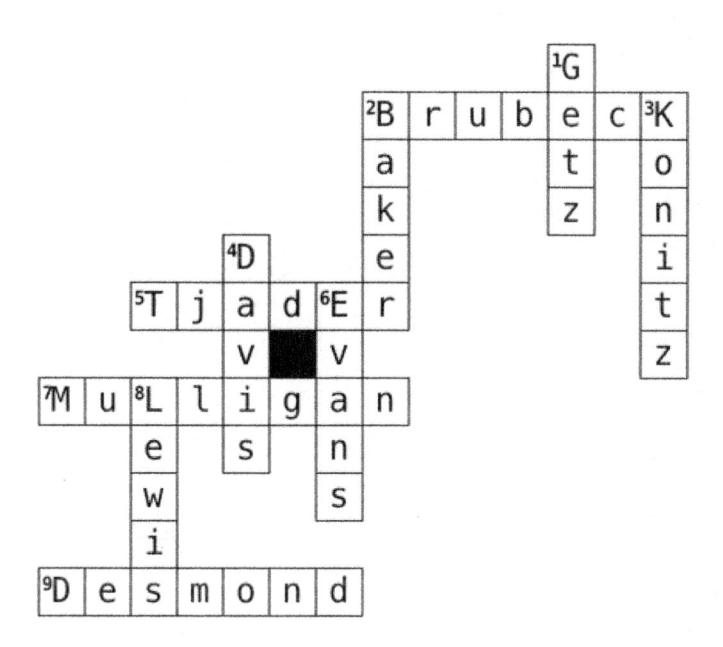

ACROSS

2. PIANIST AND COMPOSER KNOWN FOR HIS WORK IN THE COOL JAZZ GENRE.
5. VIBRAPHONIST WHO BLENDED COOL JAZZ WITH LATIN MUSIC.
7. BARITONE SAXOPHONIST KNOWN FOR HIS WORK IN COOL JAZZ.
9. SAXOPHONIST WHO COLLABORATED WITH DAVE BRUBECK, COMPOSER OF "TAKE FIVE."

DOWN

1. SAXOPHONIST KNOWN FOR HIS SMOOTH TONE AND WORK IN COOL JAZZ.
2. TRUMPETER AND VOCALIST, A KEY FIGURE IN THE COOL JAZZ MOVEMENT.
3. SAXOPHONIST WHO WAS PART OF THE "BIRTH OF THE COOL" SESSIONS.
4. TRUMPETER WHO LED THE "BIRTH OF THE COOL" SESSIONS.
6. PIANIST WHO WORKED WITH MILES DAVIS, CONTRIBUTING TO THE COOL JAZZ SOUND.
8. PIANIST AND LEADER OF THE MODERN JAZZ QUARTET, A COOL JAZZ GROUP.

THE JAZZ RHYTHM SECTION

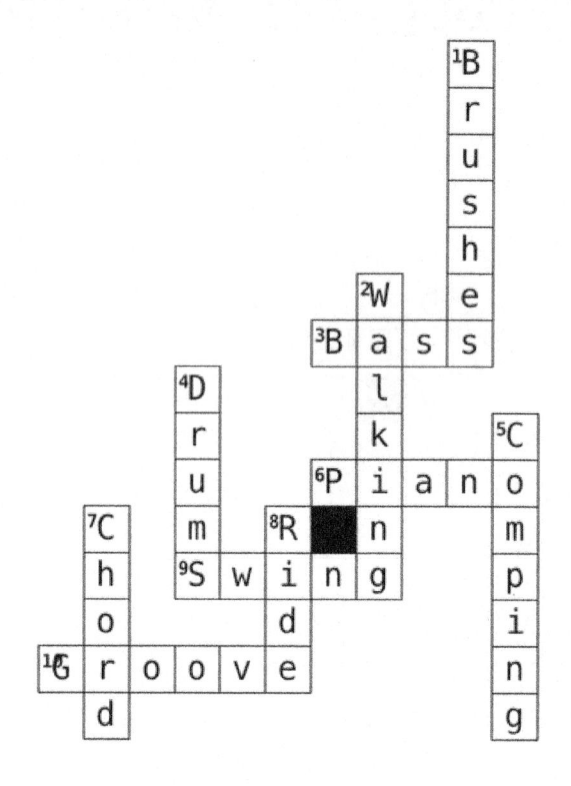

```
                    ¹B
                    r
                    u
                    s
                    h
                    e
              ²W    e
           ³B  a  s  s
       ⁴D     l
        r     k          ⁵C
        u    ⁶P  i  a  n  o
    ⁷C  m  ⁸R     n       m
     h    ⁹S  w  i  n  g  p
     o        d           i
    ¹⁰G  r  o  o  v  e    n
        d                 g
```

ACROSS

3. INSTRUMENT THAT PROVIDES THE HARMONIC FOUNDATION IN A JAZZ RHYTHM SECTION.

6. INSTRUMENT KNOWN FOR ITS VERSATILITY IN BOTH HARMONY AND MELODY IN JAZZ.

9. A STYLE OF JAZZ CHARACTERIZED BY A STRONG RHYTHMIC GROOVE AND SMOOTH PHRASING.

10. THE OVERALL FEEL OR SWING CREATED BY THE RHYTHM SECTION IN JAZZ.

DOWN

1. DRUMSTICKS WITH BRISTLES, OFTEN USED FOR SOFTER, MORE SUBTLE PLAYING.

2. A BASSLINE TECHNIQUE THAT OUTLINES THE CHORD CHANGES WITH QUARTER NOTES.

4. INSTRUMENT RESPONSIBLE FOR MAINTAINING RHYTHM AND ADDING DYNAMIC ACCENTS.

5. THE PRACTICE OF PLAYING CHORDS RHYTHMICALLY TO ACCOMPANY A SOLOIST.

7. A SET OF NOTES PLAYED TOGETHER, FORMING THE HARMONIC STRUCTURE IN JAZZ.

8. A TYPE OF CYMBAL USED IN JAZZ DRUMMING TO MAINTAIN STEADY RHYTHM.

THE WOODWINDS OF JAZZ

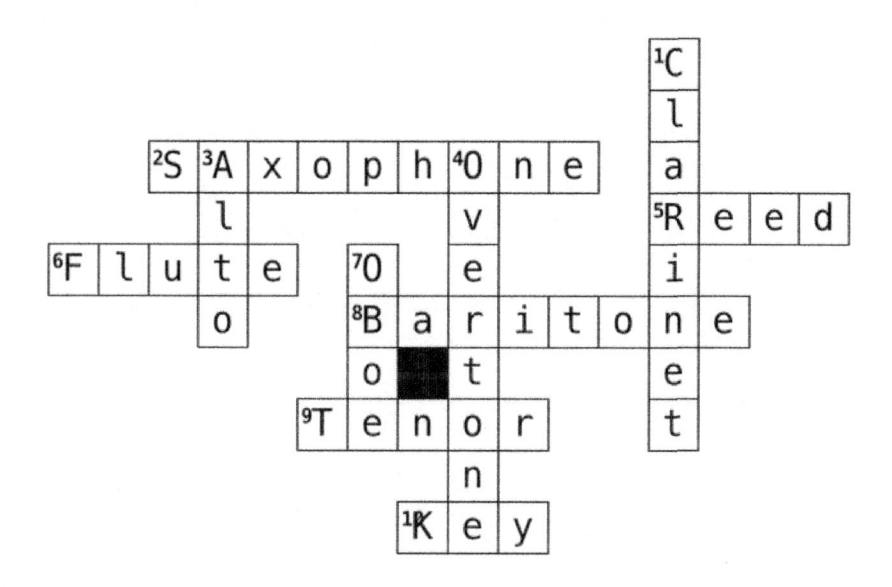

							¹C		
							l		
	²S	³A	x	o	p	h	⁴O	n	e	a
		l					v		⁵R	e	e	d
⁶F	l	u	t	e		⁷O		e		i
		o			⁸B	a	r	i	t	o	n	e
					o		t		e
			⁹T	e	n	o	r		t
					n
				¹⁰K	e	y

ACROSS

2. A WOODWIND INSTRUMENT COMMONLY ASSOCIATED WITH JAZZ, COMES IN VARIOUS SIZES.
5. A THIN PIECE OF CANE USED TO PRODUCE SOUND IN WOODWIND INSTRUMENTS.
6. A WOODWIND INSTRUMENT SOMETIMES USED IN JAZZ, KNOWN FOR ITS BRIGHT, AIRY SOUND.
8. THE LARGEST COMMON SAXOPHONE, KNOWN FOR ITS LOW, POWERFUL TONE.
9. A POPULAR TYPE OF SAXOPHONE WITH A DEEP, RICH SOUND.
10. A MECHANISM ON WOODWIND INSTRUMENTS THAT OPENS OR CLOSES HOLES TO CHANGE PITCH.

DOWN

1. A WOODWIND INSTRUMENT WITH A SINGLE REED, USED IN EARLY JAZZ AND SWING.
3. A TYPE OF SAXOPHONE, SMALLER AND HIGHER-PITCHED THAN THE TENOR.
4. A HARMONIC PRODUCED ON WOODWIND INSTRUMENTS, CONTRIBUTING TO THE INSTRUMENT'S TONE.
7. A DOUBLE-REED WOODWIND INSTRUMENT, LESS COMMON IN JAZZ BUT SOMETIMES USED.

THE BRASS IN JAZZ

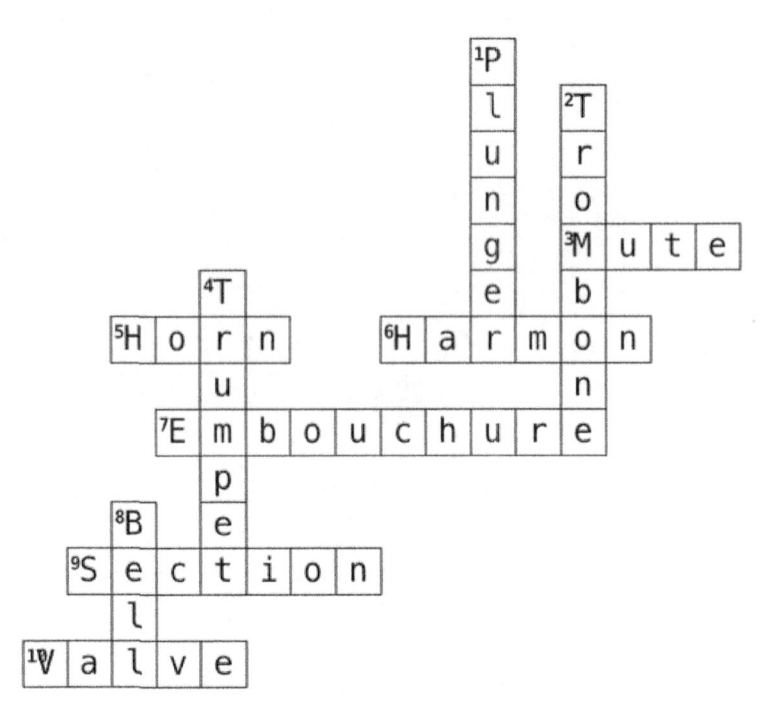

						¹P						
						l		²T				
						u		r				
						n		o				
						g		³M	u	t	e	
			⁴T			e		b				
	⁵H	o	r	n		⁶H	a	r	m	o	n	
			u					n				
		⁷E	m	b	o	u	c	h	u	r	e	
			p									
	⁸B		e									
	⁹S	e	c	t	i	o	n					
	l											
¹⁰V	a	l	v	e								

ACROSS

3. A DEVICE INSERTED INTO A BRASS INSTRUMENT TO ALTER ITS SOUND.

5. A COLLOQUIAL TERM USED FOR BRASS INSTRUMENTS LIKE TRUMPET AND TROMBONE.

6. A TYPE OF MUTE OFTEN USED BY MILES DAVIS
TO CREATE A DISTINCTIVE SOUND.

7. THE WAY A MUSICIAN APPLIES THEIR MOUTH TO THE MOUTHPIECE OF A BRASS INSTRUMENT.

9. A GROUP OF BRASS PLAYERS IN A JAZZ BAND,
OFTEN INCLUDING TRUMPETS AND TROMBONES.

10. A MECHANISM ON BRASS INSTRUMENTS THAT
ALTERS THE PITCH WHEN PRESSED.

DOWN

1. A TYPE OF MUTE THAT RESEMBLES A SINK PLUNGER, USED FOR EXPRESSIVE EFFECTS.

2. A BRASS INSTRUMENT WITH A SLIDE, KNOWN FOR ITS DEEP, RICH TONE.

4. A BRASS INSTRUMENT WITH A BRIGHT, PENETRATING SOUND, WIDELY USED IN JAZZ.

8. THE FLARED END OF A BRASS INSTRUMENT WHERE THE SOUND IS PROJECTED.

JAZZ FUSION

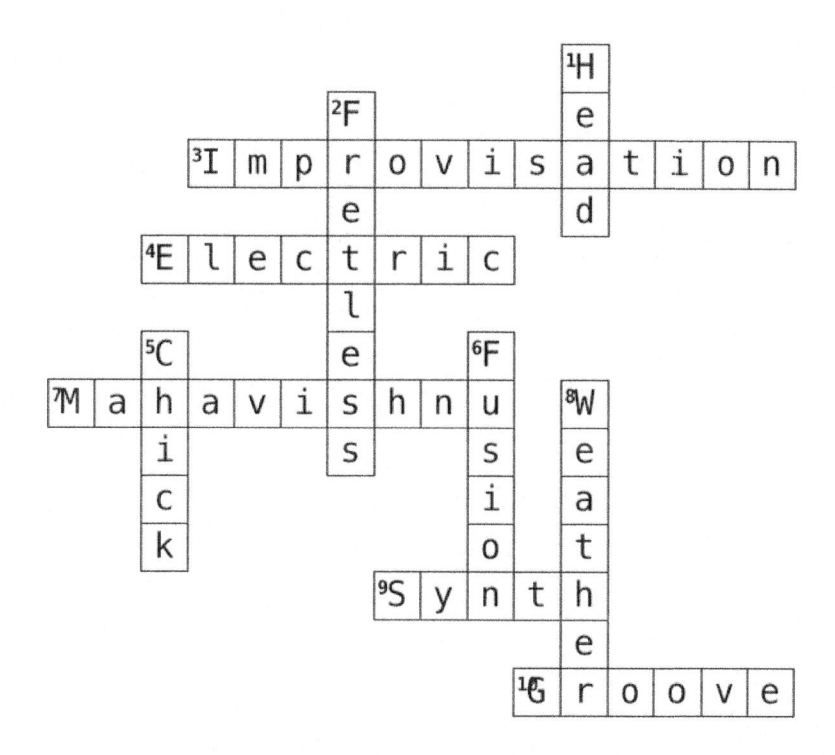

ACROSS

3. THE SPONTANEOUS CREATION OF MUSIC, A HALLMARK OF BOTH JAZZ AND FUSION.
4. REFERS TO INSTRUMENTS LIKE THE ELECTRIC GUITAR AND ELECTRIC BASS USED IN FUSION.
7. REFERS TO THE "MAHAVISHNU ORCHESTRA," A GROUP KNOWN FOR ITS FUSION OF JAZZ AND ROCK.
9. SHORT FOR SYNTHESIZER, AN ELECTRONIC INSTRUMENT USED IN JAZZ FUSION.
10. THE RHYTHMIC FEEL OR SWING, CRUCIAL IN FUSION FOR BLENDING JAZZ WITH OTHER STYLES.

DOWN

1. THE MAIN THEME OR MELODY IN A JAZZ COMPOSITION, OFTEN PLAYED BEFORE AND AFTER IMPROVISATIONS.
2. A TYPE OF BASS GUITAR WITH NO FRETS, OFTEN USED IN FUSION FOR ITS SMOOTH, SLIDING NOTES.
5. REFERS TO CHICK COREA, A KEY FIGURE IN JAZZ FUSION.
6. A STYLE OF JAZZ THAT BLENDS ELEMENTS OF ROCK, FUNK, AND OTHER GENRES.
8. REFERS TO "WEATHER REPORT," A PIONEERING JAZZ FUSION BAND.

LATIN JAZZ

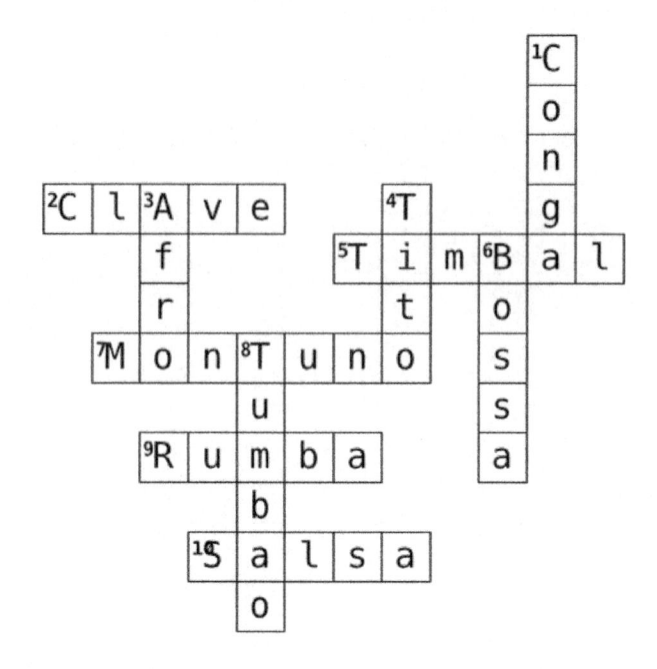

								¹C		
								o		
								n		
	²C	l	³A	v	e		⁴T	g		
			f			⁵T	i	m	⁶B	a	l
			r				t		o	
		⁷M	o	n	⁸T	u	n	o	s	
					u				s	
			⁹R	u	m	b	a		a	
					b					
				¹⁰S	a	l	s	a		
					o					

ACROSS

2. A RHYTHMIC PATTERN ESSENTIAL TO MANY AFRO-CUBAN AND LATIN JAZZ COMPOSITIONS.
5. A PAIR OF SHALLOW DRUMS PLAYED WITH STICKS, OFTEN USED IN LATIN JAZZ.
7. A REPEATED PIANO FIGURE IN LATIN JAZZ, OFTEN USED TO ACCOMPANY SOLOS.
9. A STYLE OF CUBAN MUSIC AND DANCE, INFLUENTIAL IN THE DEVELOPMENT OF LATIN JAZZ.
10. A GENRE OF MUSIC THAT COMBINES ELEMENTS OF LATIN JAZZ, AFRO-CUBAN RHYTHMS, AND DANCE.

DOWN

1. A TALL, NARROW DRUM FROM CUBA, OFTEN USED IN LATIN JAZZ.
3. REFERS TO "AFRO-CUBAN," A BLEND OF AFRICAN AND CUBAN MUSIC STYLES, CENTRAL TO LATIN JAZZ.
4. REFERS TO TITO PUENTE, A LEGENDARY FIGURE IN LATIN JAZZ.
6. REFERS TO "BOSSA NOVA," A STYLE OF BRAZILIAN MUSIC THAT BLENDS SAMBA AND JAZZ.
8. THE SYNCOPATED BASS PATTERN COMMONLY USED IN LATIN JAZZ.

JAZZ SONG TITLES

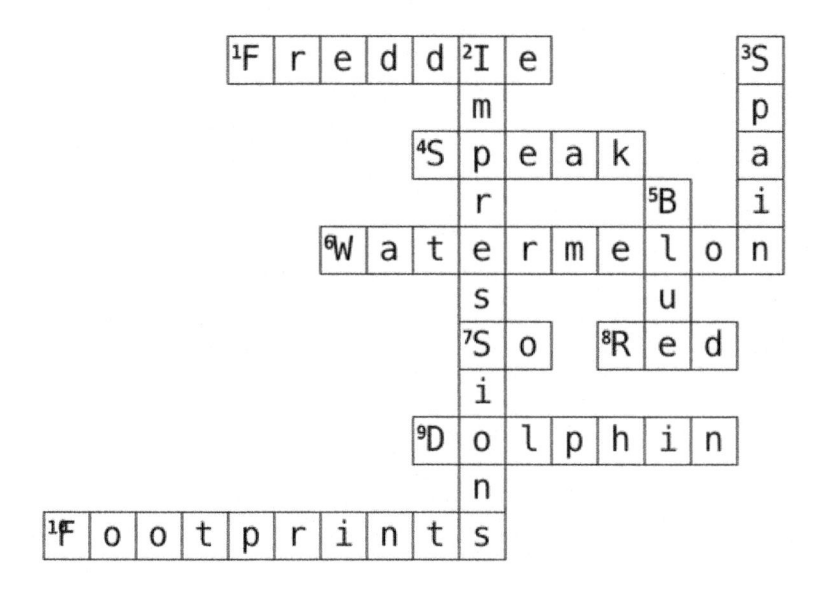

¹F	r	e	d	d	²I	e			³S	
					m				p	
			⁴S	p	e	a	k		a	
					r			⁵B	i	
			⁶W	a	t	e	r	m	e	l	o	n
					s			u		
				⁷S	o		⁸R	e	d	
				i						
			⁹D	o	l	p	h	i	n	
				n						
¹⁰F	o	o	t	p	r	i	n	t	s	

ACROSS

1. THE FIRST WORD IN THE TITLE OF A BLUESY TUNE FROM MILES DAVIS'S "KIND OF BLUE" ALBUM.
4. THE FIRST WORD IN THE TITLE OF A JAZZ STANDARD BY WAYNE SHORTER, ALSO THE NAME OF AN ALBUM.
6. THE FIRST WORD IN THE TITLE OF A FUNKY TUNE BY HERBIE HANCOCK FROM HIS EARLY BLUE NOTE RECORDINGS.
7. THE FIRST WORD IN THE TITLE OF A FAMOUS TUNE BY MILES DAVIS FROM THE ALBUM "KIND OF BLUE."
8. THE FIRST WORD IN THE TITLE OF A HARD BOP TUNE BY FREDDIE HUBBARD FROM HIS 1970 ALBUM.
9. A JAZZ PIECE BY LUIZ EÇA, KNOWN FOR ITS LYRICAL MELODY, NAMED AFTER A MARINE ANIMAL.
10. A JAZZ COMPOSITION BY WAYNE SHORTER, OFTEN PLAYED IN A 6/8 TIME SIGNATURE.

DOWN

2. A MODAL JAZZ COMPOSITION BY JOHN COLTRANE, OFTEN ASSOCIATED WITH HIS LIVE PERFORMANCES.
3. A JAZZ COMPOSITION BY CHICK COREA, KNOWN FOR ITS LIVELY RHYTHM AND SPANISH-INSPIRED MELODY.
5. THE FIRST WORD IN THE TITLE OF A BLUES COMPOSITION BY THELONIOUS MONK.

ICONIC JAZZ ALBUMS

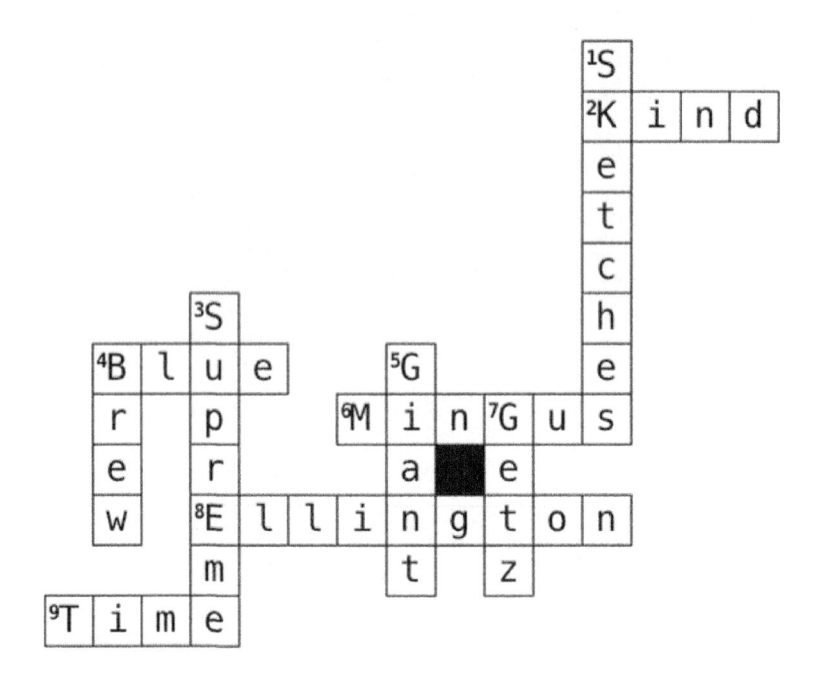

```
                                    ¹S
                                    ²K  i  n  d
                                    e
                                    t
                                    c
                                    h
               ³S                   e
        ⁴B  l  u  e        ⁵G
        r      p        ⁶M  i  n  ⁷G  u  s
        e      r            a      e
        w      ⁸E  l  l  i  n  g  t  o  n
               m            t      z
        ⁹T  i  m  e
```

ACROSS

2. THE FIRST WORD IN THE TITLE OF A LANDMARK MILES DAVIS ALBUM FROM 1959.
4. A COLOR-THEMED ALBUM BY JOHN COLTRANE FROM 1957.
6. A LEGENDARY BASSIST AND COMPOSER WHO RELEASED THE INFLUENTIAL ALBUM "AH UM" IN 1959.
8. HIS LIVE ALBUM AT NEWPORT IS ONE OF THE MOST FAMOUS JAZZ PERFORMANCES OF ALL TIME.
9. THE KEY CONCEPT EXPLORED IN DAVE BRUBECK'S GROUNDBREAKING ALBUM FEATURING "TAKE FIVE."

DOWN

1. AN ALBUM BY MILES DAVIS THAT EXPLORES SPANISH THEMES, RELEASED IN 1960.
3. A SPIRITUAL JAZZ ALBUM BY JOHN COLTRANE RELEASED IN 1965.
4. A WORD IN THE TITLE OF A PIONEERING JAZZ FUSION ALBUM BY MILES DAVIS FROM 1970.
5. THE FIRST WORD IN THE TITLE OF JOHN COLTRANE'S REVOLUTIONARY ALBUM FROM 1960.
7. LAST NAME OF THE SAXOPHONIST WHO POPULARIZED BOSSA NOVA WITH AN ALBUM FEATURING "THE GIRL FROM IPANEMA."

JAZZ STANDARDS

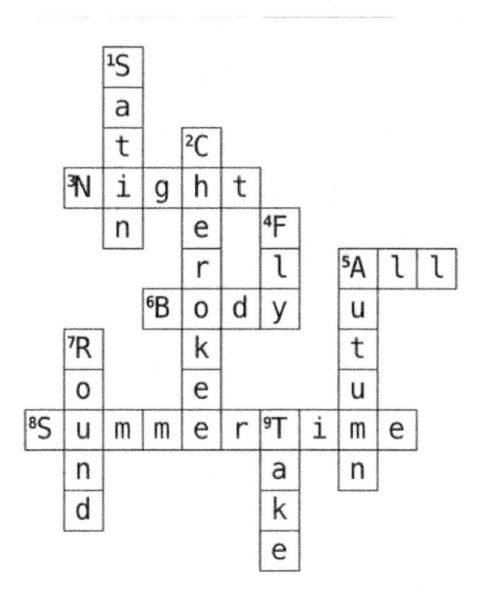

```
        ¹S
         a
         t
         u   ²C
     ³N  i g h  t
         n   e
             r   ⁴F
             l   ⁵A l l
         ⁶B o d y   u
     ⁷R      k       t
      o      e       u
     ⁸S u m m e r ⁹T i m e
      n              a
      d              k
                     e
```

ACROSS

3. THE FIRST WORD IN A POPULAR JAZZ STANDARD BY COLE PORTER THAT CONTRASTS DAY AND NIGHT.

5. THE FIRST WORD IN A JAZZ STANDARD BY JEROME KERN, OFTEN PLAYED IN MAJOR AND MINOR KEYS.

6. A CLASSIC JAZZ BALLAD THAT HAS BEEN A FAVORITE FOR IMPROVISATION BY JAZZ MUSICIANS.

8. A JAZZ STANDARD FROM AN OPERA BY GEORGE GERSHWIN, OFTEN COVERED BY JAZZ MUSICIANS.

DOWN

1. THE FIRST WORD IN A JAZZ STANDARD FAMOUSLY PERFORMED BY SARAH VAUGHAN AND ELLA FITZGERALD.

2. A FAST-PACED JAZZ STANDARD OFTEN USED AS A TEST PIECE FOR IMPROVISATION.

4. THE FIRST WORD IN A JAZZ SONG POPULARIZED BY FRANK SINATRA THAT TALKS ABOUT THE MOON.

5. THE FIRST WORD IN THE TITLE OF A JAZZ STANDARD OFTEN ASSOCIATED WITH THE FALL SEASON.

7. THE FIRST WORD IN A CLASSIC JAZZ BALLAD BY THELONIOUS MONK.

9. THE FIRST WORD IN THE TITLE OF A POPULAR JAZZ PIECE COMPOSED BY PAUL DESMOND, KNOWN FOR ITS 5/4 TIME SIGNATURE.

THE GREAT COMPOSERS

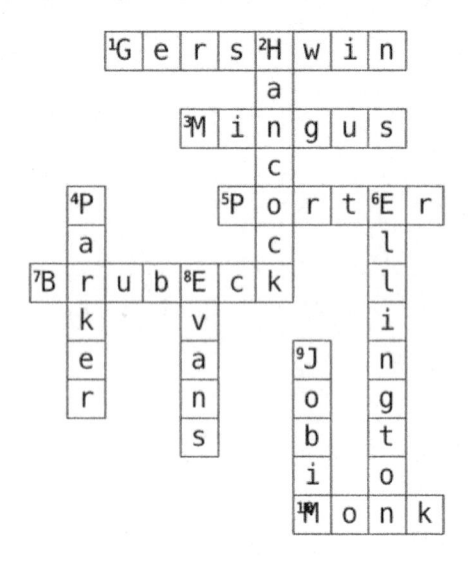

				¹G	e	r	s	²H	w	i	n	
								a				
						³M	i	n	g	u	s	
								c				
		⁴P			⁵P	o	r	t	⁶E	r		
		a				c			l			
⁷B	r	u	b	⁸E	c	k			l			
k		e		v					i			
e		r		a			⁹J		n			
r				n			o		g			
				s			b		t			
							i		o			
							¹⁰M	o	n	k	

ACROSS

1. LAST NAME OF THE COMPOSER WHO MERGED JAZZ WITH CLASSICAL MUSIC IN WORKS LIKE "RHAPSODY IN BLUE."
3. LAST NAME OF THE BASSIST AND COMPOSER KNOWN FOR HIS COMPLEX COMPOSITIONS AND SOCIAL COMMENTARY IN PIECES LIKE "FABLES OF FAUBUS."
5. LAST NAME OF THE COMPOSER OF MANY JAZZ STANDARDS, INCLUDING "ANYTHING GOES" AND "NIGHT AND DAY."
7. LAST NAME OF THE COMPOSER AND PIANIST WHO EXPERIMENTED WITH UNUSUAL TIME SIGNATURES IN PIECES LIKE "BLUE RONDO À LA TURK."
10. LAST NAME OF A JAZZ COMPOSER KNOWN FOR HIS ANGULAR MELODIES AND COMPOSITIONS LIKE "'ROUND MIDNIGHT."

DOWN

2. LAST NAME OF THE PIANIST AND COMPOSER KNOWN FOR INTEGRATING FUNK AND ELECTRONIC ELEMENTS INTO JAZZ WITH ALBUMS LIKE "HEADHUNTERS."
4. LAST NAME OF THE SAXOPHONIST AND COMPOSER WHO WAS A LEADING FIGURE IN THE BEBOP MOVEMENT.
6. LAST NAME OF THE COMPOSER AND BANDLEADER KNOWN FOR "MOOD INDIGO" AND "IT DON'T MEAN A THING (IF IT AIN'T GOT THAT SWING)."
8. LAST NAME OF THE PIANIST AND COMPOSER WHOSE WORK, INCLUDING "WALTZ FOR DEBBY," HAS INFLUENCED GENERATIONS OF JAZZ MUSICIANS.
9. LAST NAME OF THE BRAZILIAN COMPOSER WHO WROTE "THE GIRL FROM IPANEMA," POPULARIZING BOSSA NOVA WORLDWIDE.

LIVE JAZZ RECORDINGS

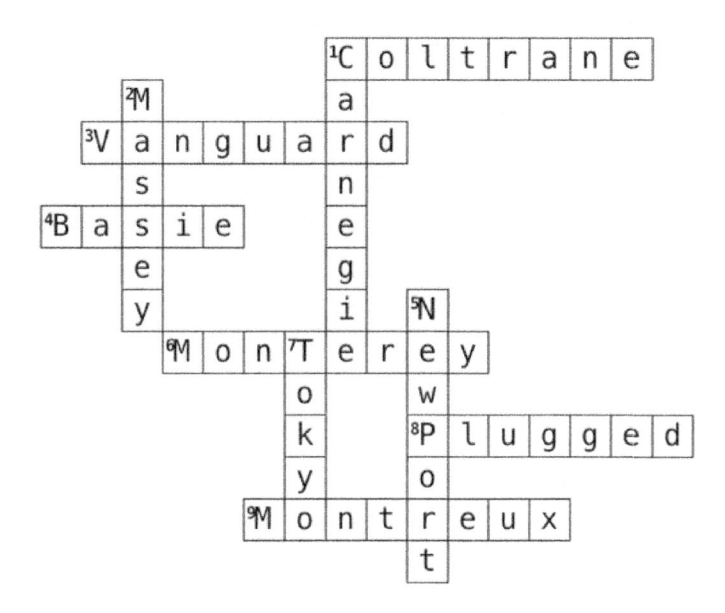

```
            ¹C o l t r a n e
        ²M  a
     ³V a n g u a r d
        s   n
   ⁴B a s i e   e
        e       g
        y       i   ⁵N
            ⁶M o n ⁷T e r e y
                   o   w
                   k   ⁸P l u g g e d
                   y   o
                ⁹M o n t r e u x
                       t
```

ACROSS

1. THE LAST NAME OF THE SAXOPHONIST WHO RECORDED A LANDMARK LIVE ALBUM AT THE VILLAGE VANGUARD IN 1961.
3. A FAMOUS JAZZ CLUB IN NEW YORK CITY WHERE BILL EVANS RECORDED A LIVE ALBUM IN 1961.
4. THE LAST NAME OF THE BANDLEADER WHOSE PERFORMANCE AT THE NEWPORT JAZZ FESTIVAL IN 1957 BECAME A FAMOUS LIVE RECORDING. 6. A JAZZ FESTIVAL IN CALIFORNIA WHERE THELONIOUS MONK GAVE A MEMORABLE PERFORMANCE, LATER RELEASED AS A LIVE ALBUM.
8. A WORD FROM THE TITLE OF A LIVE ALBUM BY MILES DAVIS, RECORDED AT THE FILLMORE EAST.
9. A SWISS JAZZ FESTIVAL WHERE ELLA FITZGERALD'S LIVE PERFORMANCE WAS CAPTURED ON A CELEBRATED ALBUM.

DOWN

1. A PRESTIGIOUS CONCERT HALL IN NEW YORK CITY WHERE BENNY GOODMAN PERFORMED A LEGENDARY JAZZ CONCERT IN 1938.
2. A FAMOUS LIVE JAZZ RECORDING VENUE IN TORONTO WHERE A HISTORIC JAZZ CONCERT TOOK PLACE IN 1953.
5. THE LOCATION OF A FAMOUS JAZZ FESTIVAL WHERE DUKE ELLINGTON REVIVED HIS CAREER WITH A HISTORIC 1956 PERFORMANCE.
7. A CITY WHERE MILES DAVIS RECORDED A LIVE ALBUM FEATURING HIS 1964 QUINTET.

THE BIRTH OF JAZZ

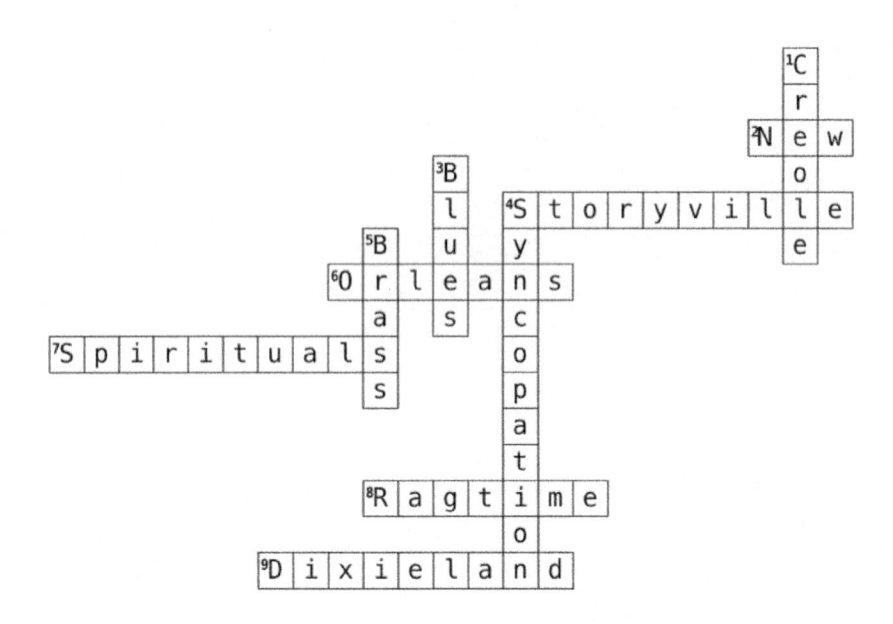

```
                                        ¹C
                                         r
                                ²N  e  w
                                         o
                    ³B                   
                    l       ⁴S t o r y v i l l e
              ⁵B    u                    e
           ⁶O  r  l e  a  n  s
              a     s       y
    ⁷S p i r i t  u  a  l  s    c
              s             o
                            p
                            a
                            t
                 ⁸R  a  g   t  i  m  e
                            o
                 ⁹D  i  x   i  e  l  a  n  d
```

ACROSS

2. THE FIRST WORD IN THE NAME OF THE CITY WHERE JAZZ IS OFTEN SAID TO HAVE ORIGINATED.

4. THE RED-LIGHT DISTRICT IN NEW ORLEANS WHERE EARLY JAZZ MUSICIANS OFTEN PERFORMED.

6. THE CITY WHERE JAZZ MUSIC BEGAN TO FLOURISH IN THE EARLY 20TH CENTURY.

7. RELIGIOUS SONGS THAT INFLUENCED EARLY JAZZ AND BLUES, OFTEN SUNG BY AFRICAN AMERICAN COMMUNITIES.

8. A PRECURSOR TO JAZZ, THIS PIANO-BASED MUSIC STYLE WAS POPULAR IN THE LATE 19TH AND EARLY 20TH CENTURIES.

9. A STYLE OF JAZZ THAT ORIGINATED IN NEW ORLEANS, CHARACTERIZED BY A COLLECTIVE IMPROVISATION.

DOWN

1. A CULTURAL GROUP IN NEW ORLEANS WHOSE MUSICAL TRADITIONS CONTRIBUTED TO THE BIRTH OF JAZZ.

3. A GENRE OF MUSIC THAT GREATLY INFLUENCED THE DEVELOPMENT OF JAZZ, CHARACTERIZED BY ITS 12-BAR STRUCTURE.

4. A RHYTHMIC CONCEPT WHERE THE EMPHASIS IS PLACED ON THE OFF-BEATS, A KEY ELEMENT IN JAZZ.

5. A TYPE OF BAND THAT WAS CENTRAL TO THE EARLY DEVELOPMENT OF JAZZ IN NEW ORLEANS.

JAZZ IN THE 1920S

```
            ¹R
   ²F    ³C o t t o n
   l  ⁴R    h      a
   a  e     i  ⁵P r o h i b i t i o n
   p  n     c      i
  ⁶S p e a k e a s y n
   e  i     g      g
  ⁷A r m s t r o n g
         s
         a
  ⁸E l l i n g t o n
         c
  ⁹H a r l e m
```

ACROSS

3. THE NAME OF A FAMOUS JAZZ CLUB IN HARLEM WHERE DUKE ELLINGTON AND OTHER LEGENDS PERFORMED.

5. THE U.S. LAW THAT BANNED ALCOHOL IN THE 1920S, LEADING TO THE RISE OF SPEAKEASIES WHERE JAZZ THRIVED.

6. AN ILLEGAL BAR DURING PROHIBITION WHERE JAZZ MUSIC WAS OFTEN PLAYED.

7. THE LAST NAME OF THE TRUMPETER WHO BECAME ONE OF THE MOST INFLUENTIAL FIGURES IN JAZZ DURING THE 1920S. 8. A JAZZ COMPOSER AND BANDLEADER WHO ROSE TO FAME DURING THE 1920S.

9. A NEW YORK NEIGHBORHOOD THAT BECAME THE EPICENTER OF JAZZ CULTURE IN THE 1920S.

DOWN

1. A TERM USED TO DESCRIBE THE 1920S, AN ERA MARKED BY ECONOMIC PROSPERITY AND CULTURAL CHANGE, INCLUDING THE RISE OF JAZZ.

2. A TERM FOR THE YOUNG, FASHIONABLE WOMEN OF THE 1920S WHO WERE OFTEN ASSOCIATED WITH JAZZ CLUBS.

3. A CITY THAT BECAME A MAJOR HUB FOR JAZZ MUSICIANS AFTER MANY MIGRATED FROM NEW ORLEANS.

4. THE CULTURAL MOVEMENT IN HARLEM DURING THE 1920S THAT GREATLY INFLUENCED JAZZ.

JAZZ CLUBS AND VENUES

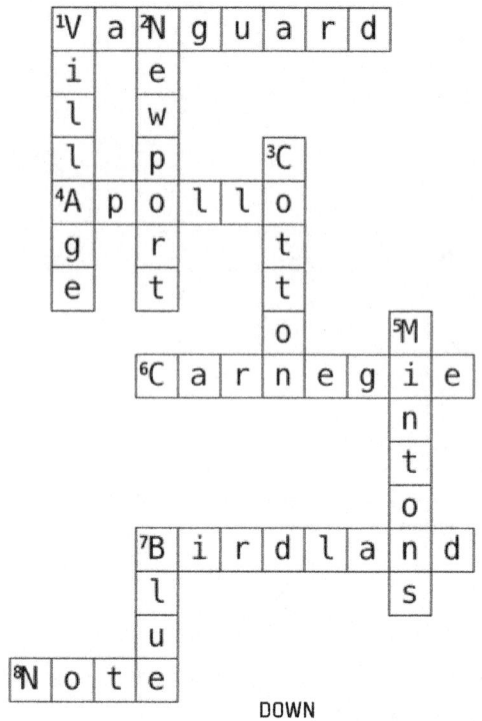

¹V	a	²N	g	u	a	r	d		
i		e							
l		w							
l		p			³C				
⁴A	p	o	l	l	o				
g		r			t				
e		t			t				
					o		⁵M		
				⁶C	a	r	n	e	g	i	e
							n		
							t		
							o		
			⁷B	i	r	d	l	a	n	d
			l				s		
			u						
		⁸N	o	t	e				

ACROSS

1. THE SECOND WORD IN THE NAME OF THE ICONIC JAZZ CLUB IN GREENWICH VILLAGE.
4. A HISTORIC THEATER IN HARLEM KNOWN FOR ITS JAZZ AND SOUL MUSIC PERFORMANCES.
6. A PRESTIGIOUS CONCERT HALL IN NEW YORK WHERE BENNY GOODMAN PLAYED A FAMOUS JAZZ CONCERT.
7. A FAMOUS NEW YORK JAZZ CLUB NAMED AFTER CHARLIE PARKER, KNOWN AS "BIRD".
8. THE SECOND WORD IN THE NAME OF THE ICONIC JAZZ CLUB IN GREENWICH VILLAGE.

DOWN

1. THE FIRST WORD IN THE NAME OF A FAMOUS JAZZ CLUB IN NEW YORK'S GREENWICH VILLAGE.
2. A RHODE ISLAND JAZZ FESTIVAL VENUE WHERE DUKE ELLINGTON REVITALIZED HIS CAREER IN 1956.
3. THE FIRST WORD IN THE NAME OF A FAMOUS HARLEM CLUB WHERE MANY JAZZ LEGENDS PERFORMED.
5. A JAZZ CLUB IN HARLEM THAT WAS A BIRTHPLACE OF THE BEBOP MOVEMENT.
7. THE FIRST WORD IN THE NAME OF A FAMOUS JAZZ CLUB IN NEW YORK, KNOWN FOR ITS BLUE-THEMED DECOR.

JAZZ FESTIVALS

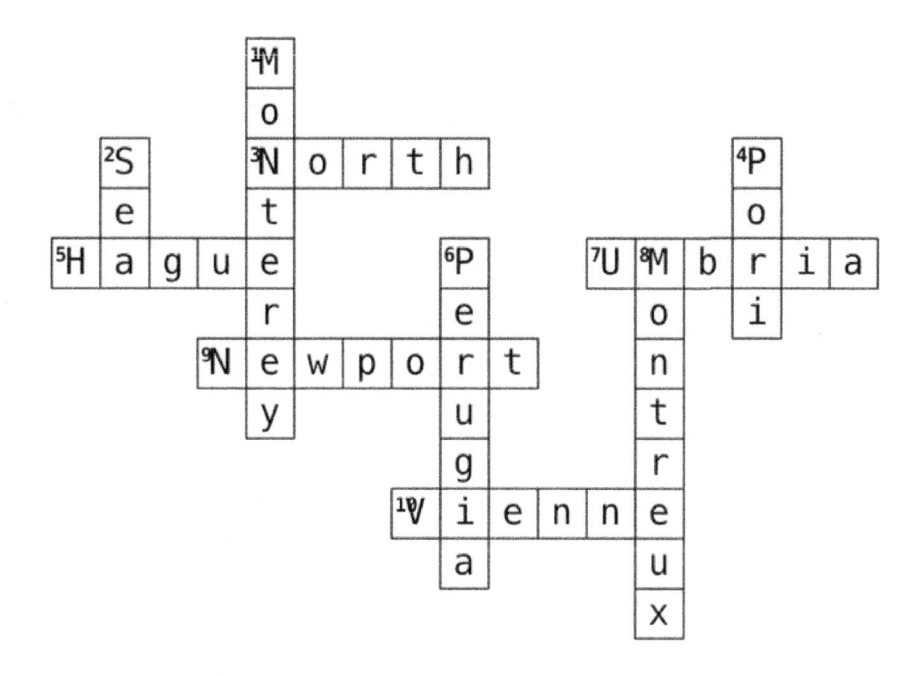

			¹M									
			o									
	²S		³N	o	r	t	h		⁴P			
	e		t						o			
⁵H	a	g	u	e		⁶P		⁷U	⁸M	b	r	i	a
	r					e			o		i	
	⁹N	e	w	p	o	r	t		n			
	y					u			t			
						g			r			
				¹⁰V	i	e	n	n	e			
						a			u			
									x			

ACROSS

3. THE FIRST WORD IN THE NAME OF A FAMOUS JAZZ FESTIVAL HELD IN CHICAGO SINCE 1959.
5. A DUTCH CITY WHERE THE NORTH SEA JAZZ FESTIVAL WAS ORIGINALLY HELD.
7. AN ITALIAN REGION KNOWN FOR ITS ANNUAL JAZZ FESTIVAL, ONE OF EUROPE'S MOST PRESTIGIOUS.
9. THE RHODE ISLAND FESTIVAL WHERE DUKE ELLINGTON MADE A HISTORIC COMEBACK IN 1956.
10. A FRENCH TOWN KNOWN FOR ITS ANNUAL JAZZ FESTIVAL IN A ROMAN AMPHITHEATER.

DOWN

1. A CALIFORNIA JAZZ FESTIVAL KNOWN FOR ITS DIVERSE LINE-UP AND OUTDOOR SETTING.
2. THE SECOND WORD IN THE NAME OF THE JAZZ FESTIVAL HELD ANNUALLY IN SEATTLE.
4. A FINNISH CITY THAT HOSTS ONE OF THE OLDEST AND MOST RENOWNED JAZZ FESTIVALS IN EUROPE.
6. THE CITY IN ITALY WHERE THE UMBRIA JAZZ FESTIVAL IS HELD EVERY SUMMER.
8. A FAMOUS JAZZ FESTIVAL HELD ANNUALLY IN SWITZERLAND ON THE SHORES OF LAKE GENEVA.

JAZZ AND CINEMA

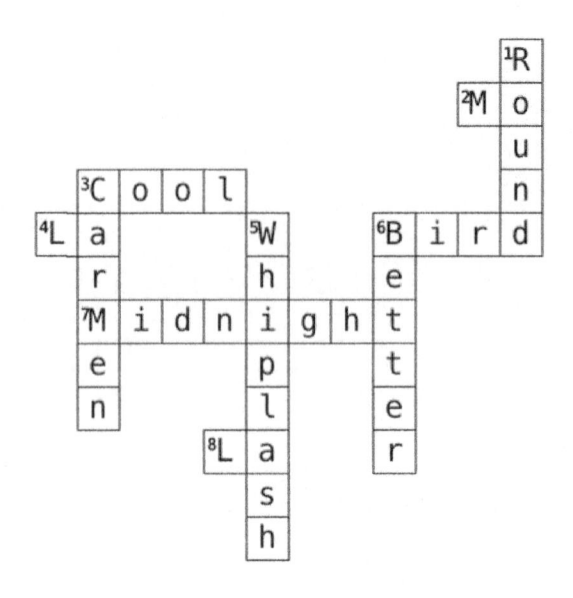

ACROSS

2. THE FIRST WORD IN THE TITLE OF A SPIKE LEE FILM CENTERED AROUND JAZZ AND A FAMILY IN BROOKLYN.
3. THE FIRST WORD IN THE TITLE OF A JAZZ CONCERT FILM BY BERT STERN, DOCUMENTING THE 1958 NEWPORT JAZZ FESTIVAL.
4. THE SECOND WORD IN THE TITLE OF THE 2016 FILM MENTIONED ABOVE.
6. A BIOGRAPHICAL FILM DIRECTED BY CLINT EASTWOOD ABOUT THE LIFE OF CHARLIE PARKER.
7. THE SECOND WORD IN THE TITLE OF A 1986 FILM ABOUT A JAZZ SAXOPHONIST IN PARIS.
8. THE FIRST WORD IN THE TITLE OF A 2016 FILM THAT PAYS HOMAGE TO JAZZ MUSIC AND HOLLYWOOD MUSICALS.

DOWN

1. THE FIRST WORD IN THE TITLE OF A MOVIE ABOUT A JAZZ MUSICIAN STRUGGLING WITH ADDICTION, STARRING DEXTER GORDON.
3. A JAZZ OPERA FILM BY OTTO PREMINGER, STARRING DOROTHY DANDRIDGE AND HARRY BELAFONTE.
5. A FILM ABOUT A YOUNG DRUMMER AND HIS INTENSE JAZZ INSTRUCTOR, RELEASED IN 2014.
6. THE FIRST WORD IN THE TITLE OF A 1984 FILM THAT TELLS THE STORY OF A JAZZ MUSICIAN AND HIS RELATIONSHIP WITH A SINGER.

EUROPEAN JAZZ

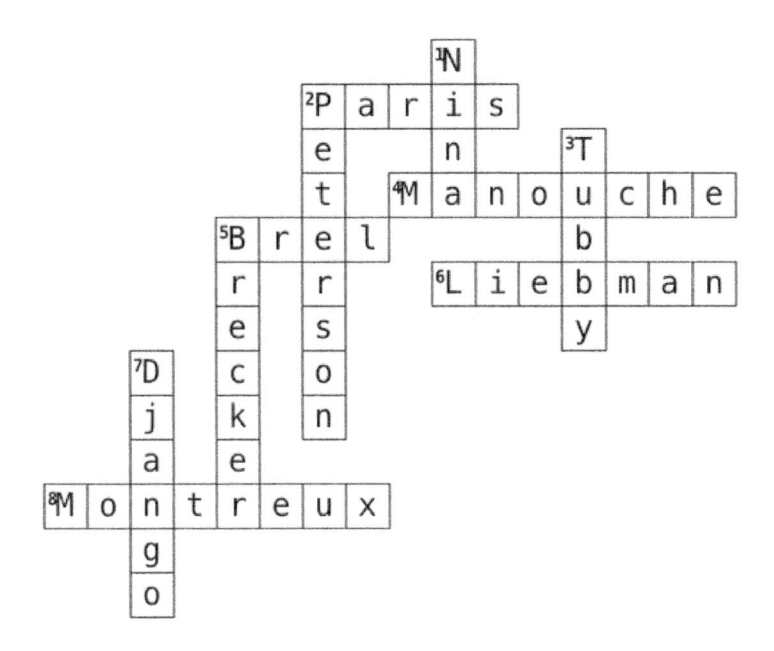

```
            ¹N
        ²P a r i s
            e   n   ³T
            t  ⁴M a n o u c h e
         ⁵B r e l       b
            r   r   ⁶L i e b m a n
            e   s       y
        ⁷D  c   o
            j  k   n
            a  e
       ⁸M o n t r e u x
            g
            o
```

ACROSS

2. THE CITY WHERE AMERICAN JAZZ MUSICIANS LIKE SIDNEY BECHET AND JOSEPHINE BAKER FOUND FAME IN THE 1920S.
4. THE STYLE OF JAZZ ASSOCIATED WITH DJANGO REINHARDT, ALSO KNOWN AS GYPSY JAZZ.
5. THE LAST NAME OF THE BELGIAN SINGER-SONGWRITER WHOSE MUSIC OFTEN INCORPORATED JAZZ ELEMENTS.
6. THE LAST NAME OF THE AMERICAN JAZZ SAXOPHONIST WHO BECAME A PROMINENT FIGURE IN EUROPEAN JAZZ EDUCATION.
8. A SWISS CITY KNOWN FOR ITS FAMOUS JAZZ FESTIVAL ON THE SHORES OF LAKE GENEVA.

DOWN

1. THE FIRST NAME OF THE FAMOUS SINGER SIMONE, WHO SPENT MUCH OF HER LATER CAREER IN EUROPE.
2. THE LAST NAME OF THE CANADIAN JAZZ PIANIST WHO WAS A STAPLE IN EUROPEAN JAZZ FESTIVALS.
3. THE FIRST NAME OF THE BRITISH SAXOPHONIST HAYES, A PIONEER OF MODERN JAZZ IN THE UK.
5. THE LAST NAME OF THE AMERICAN SAXOPHONIST MICHAEL, WHO FREQUENTLY COLLABORATED WITH EUROPEAN JAZZ ARTISTS.
7. THE FIRST NAME OF THE LEGENDARY GYPSY JAZZ GUITARIST REINHARDT.

LATIN AMERICAN JAZZ

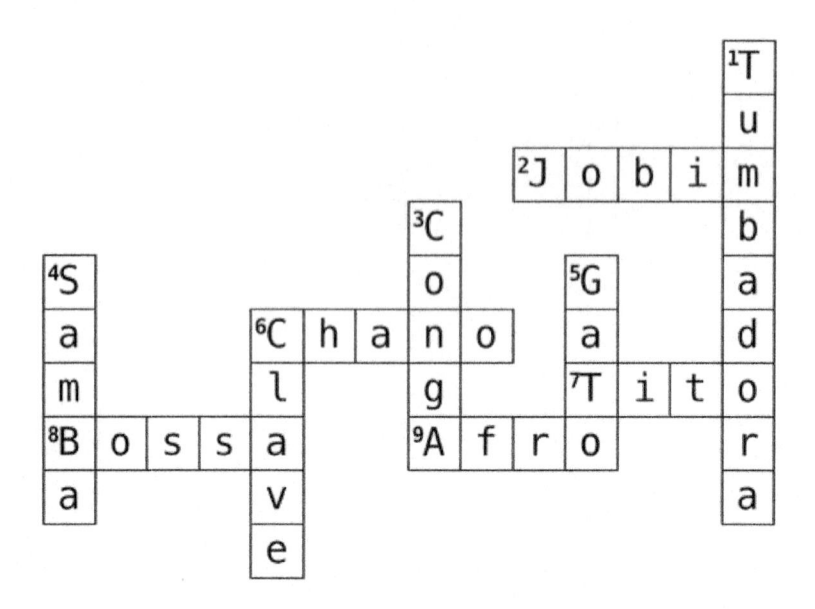

								¹T
								u
				²J	o	b	i	m
			³C					b
⁴S			o		⁵G			a
a		⁶C	h	a	n	o		d
m		l		g	⁷T	i	t	o
⁸B	o	s	s	a	⁹A	f	r	o
a		v						r
		e						a

ACROSS

2. THE LAST NAME OF THE BRAZILIAN COMPOSER WHO WROTE "THE GIRL FROM IPANEMA."
6. THE FIRST NAME OF THE CUBAN PERCUSSIONIST POZO, WHO COLLABORATED WITH DIZZY GILLESPIE.
7. THE FIRST NAME OF THE LEGENDARY LATIN JAZZ MUSICIAN PUENTE, KNOWN FOR HIS MASTERY OF THE TIMBALES.
8. A STYLE OF BRAZILIAN MUSIC THAT BLENDS SAMBA RHYTHMS WITH JAZZ HARMONY.
9. THE FIRST PART OF A TERM DESCRIBING THE BLEND OF AFRICAN AND CUBAN MUSIC THAT HEAVILY INFLUENCES LATIN JAZZ.

DOWN

1. ANOTHER TERM FOR THE CONGA DRUM, OFTEN USED IN LATIN JAZZ.
3. A TALL, NARROW DRUM FROM CUBA, COMMONLY USED IN LATIN JAZZ.
4. A BRAZILIAN DANCE AND MUSIC STYLE THAT HAS INFLUENCED MANY JAZZ MUSICIANS.
5. THE NICKNAME OF THE ARGENTINE SAXOPHONIST BARBIERI, FAMOUS FOR HIS LATIN JAZZ RECORDINGS.
6. A RHYTHMIC PATTERN ESSENTIAL TO AFRO-CUBAN MUSIC AND LATIN JAZZ.

AFRICAN JAZZ

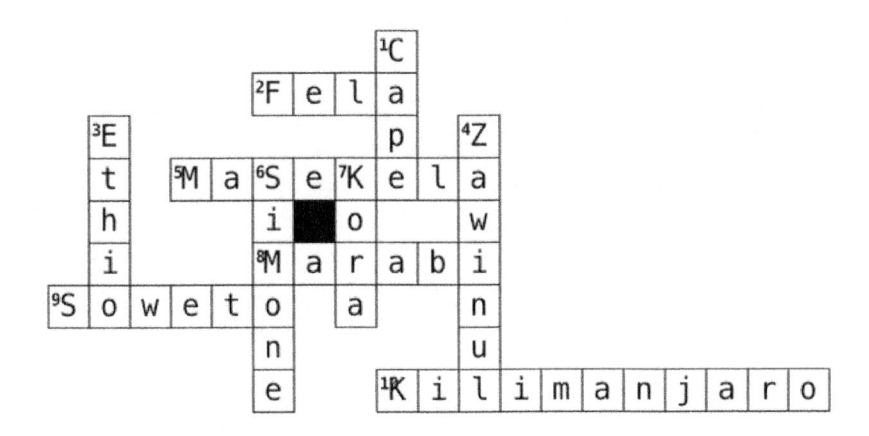

				¹C						
		²F	e	l	a					
	³E				p		⁴Z			
	t		⁵M	a	⁶S	e	⁷K	e	l	a
	h				i		o			
	i		⁸M	a	r	a	b	i		
⁹S	o	w	e	t	o		i			
					n		n			
					e		¹⁰K	i	l	i	m	a	n	j	a	r	o

ACROSS

2. THE FIRST NAME OF THE NIGERIAN MUSICIAN KUTI, WHO BLENDED JAZZ WITH AFRICAN RHYTHMS TO CREATE AFROBEAT.
5. THE LAST NAME OF THE SOUTH AFRICAN TRUMPETER WHO BECAME AN INTERNATIONAL JAZZ STAR.
8. A SOUTH AFRICAN MUSIC STYLE THAT INFLUENCED THE DEVELOPMENT OF JAZZ IN THE COUNTRY.
9. A TOWNSHIP IN SOUTH AFRICA KNOWN FOR ITS JAZZ MUSICIANS AND RICH MUSICAL HERITAGE.
10. A MOUNTAIN IN TANZANIA THAT INSPIRED A FAMOUS JAZZ TUNE BY THE JAZZ MESSENGERS.

DOWN

1. THE FIRST WORD IN THE NAME OF THE SOUTH AFRICAN CITY WITH A VIBRANT JAZZ SCENE.
3. THE FIRST PART OF A TERM USED TO DESCRIBE THE UNIQUE JAZZ STYLE THAT DEVELOPED IN ETHIOPIA.
4. THE LAST NAME OF THE AUSTRIAN KEYBOARDIST JOE, WHO INCORPORATED AFRICAN RHYTHMS INTO HIS MUSIC WITH WEATHER REPORT.
6. THE LAST NAME OF THE AMERICAN JAZZ SINGER WHO DREW INSPIRATION FROM AFRICAN MUSIC AND RHYTHMS.
7. A WEST AFRICAN STRINGED INSTRUMENT, SOMETIMES USED IN JAZZ FUSION.

ASIAN JAZZ FUSION

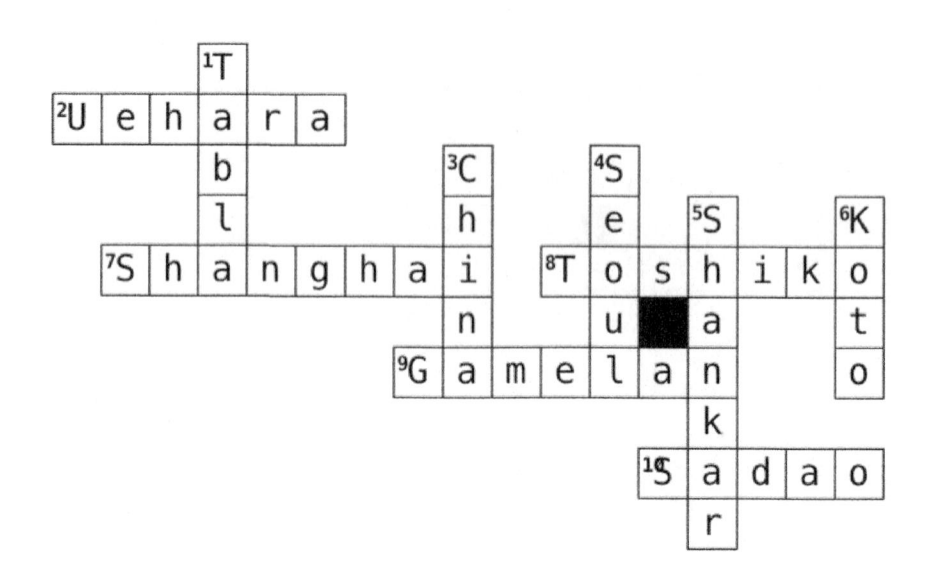

```
        ¹T
²U  e  h  a  r  a
        b        ³C        ⁴S
        l        h         e     ⁵S        ⁶K
        ⁷S  h  a  n  g  h  a  i   ⁸T  o  s  h  i  k  o
                         n         u  ■  a              t
                        ⁹G  a  m  e  l  a  n           o
                                         k
                                        ¹⁰S  a  d  a  o
                                         r
```

ACROSS

2. THE LAST NAME OF THE JAPANESE PIANIST HIROMI, KNOWN FOR HER BLEND OF JAZZ, CLASSICAL, AND ROCK.
7. A CITY IN CHINA THAT BECAME A HOTSPOT FOR JAZZ IN THE 1930S.
8. THE FIRST NAME OF THE JAPANESE JAZZ PIANIST AKIYOSHI, WHO FORMED A BIG BAND IN THE UNITED STATES.
9. A TRADITIONAL ENSEMBLE MUSIC FROM INDONESIA, SOMETIMES BLENDED WITH JAZZ ELEMENTS.
10. THE FIRST NAME OF THE JAPANESE SAXOPHONIST WATANABE, A PIONEER OF JAZZ IN ASIA.

DOWN

1. A PAIR OF DRUMS FROM INDIA, OFTEN USED IN JAZZ FUSION.
3. THE FIRST WORD IN THE TITLE OF A POPULAR JAZZ TUNE BY THELONIOUS MONK, INSPIRED BY EASTERN MUSIC.
4. THE CAPITAL OF SOUTH KOREA, WHERE A VIBRANT JAZZ SCENE HAS DEVELOPED.
5. THE LAST NAME OF THE INDIAN SITAR MAESTRO WHO INFLUENCED JAZZ MUSICIANS LIKE JOHN COLTRANE.
6. A TRADITIONAL JAPANESE STRINGED INSTRUMENT SOMETIMES INCORPORATED INTO JAZZ.

JAZZ IN AUSTRALIA AND NEW ZEALAND

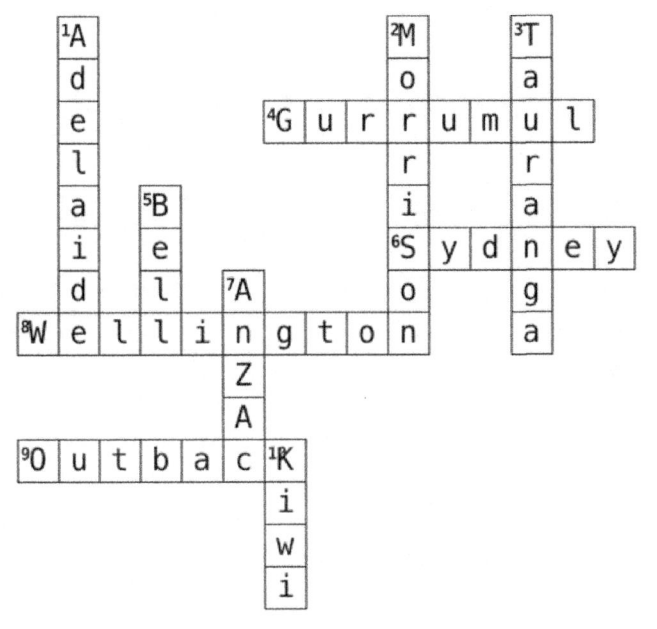

```
        ¹A              ²M      ³T
        d               o       a
        e           ⁴G  u  r  r  u  m  l
        l               r       r
        a       ⁵B      i       a
        i       e          ⁶S  y  d  n  e  y
        d       l   ⁷A     o       g
     ⁸W  e  l  l  i  n  g  t  o  n  a
                    Z
                    A
     ⁹O  u  t  b  a  c  ¹⁰K
                        i
                        w
                        i
```

ACROSS

4. THE FIRST NAME OF THE INDIGENOUS AUSTRALIAN MUSICIAN WHO INCORPORATED JAZZ ELEMENTS INTO HIS MUSIC.
6. THE AUSTRALIAN CITY THAT HOSTS ONE OF THE COUNTRY'S BIGGEST JAZZ FESTIVALS.
8. THE CAPITAL OF NEW ZEALAND, KNOWN FOR ITS VIBRANT MUSIC AND ARTS SCENE, INCLUDING JAZZ.
9. A TERM OFTEN ASSOCIATED WITH AUSTRALIA, SOMETIMES USED IN JAZZ COMPOSITIONS TO EVOKE THE VAST, REMOTE INTERIOR OF THE COUNTRY.

DOWN

1. AN AUSTRALIAN CITY KNOWN FOR ITS ANNUAL JAZZ FESTIVAL, ATTRACTING INTERNATIONAL ARTISTS.
2. THE LAST NAME OF THE AUSTRALIAN MULTI-INSTRUMENTALIST JAMES, KNOWN FOR HIS CONTRIBUTIONS TO JAZZ.
3. A CITY IN NEW ZEALAND THAT HOSTS A PROMINENT JAZZ FESTIVAL EACH YEAR.
5. THE LAST NAME OF THE AUSTRALIAN JAZZ MUSICIAN GRAEME, CONSIDERED A PIONEER OF TRADITIONAL JAZZ IN AUSTRALIA.
7. THE ACRONYM REPRESENTING THE COLLABORATION BETWEEN AUSTRALIAN AND NEW ZEALAND MUSICIANS, INCLUDING IN JAZZ.
10. A NICKNAME FOR SOMEONE FROM NEW ZEALAND, A COUNTRY WITH A GROWING JAZZ SCENE.

ENJOYED SOLVING THESE CROSSWORDS? WE'D LOVE TO HEAR YOUR THOUGHTS—PLEASE LEAVE A REVIEW AND LET US KNOW HOW WE DID!

@MOLLYMCMANUS

Printed in Great Britain
by Amazon